JULIE GAUTHIER

HUNGRY TO BE ME

A QUEST TO BE MY OWN HERO

Hungry to Be Me

A Quest To Be My Own Hero

Julie Gauthier
AUTHOR | RECOVERY ADVOCATE | YOGI

Daring to Share Global

Published by Julie Gauthier
November 2021 ISBN: 9781777939700

Editor: Diana Reyers
Typeset: Greg Salisbury
Book Cover Design: Julie Gauthier
Photography: Summer & Co. Photography

For my sister, Stéphanie

Testimonials

Eating disorders continue to pose a serious threat to the health and well-being of many Canadians. Women and girls especially are targeted by cultural messages about beauty and thinness that manifest all too often in body dysmorphia and life-threatening relationships with food. One critical step toward eliminating this pernicious and insidious social problem is to expose it to the light – to address it openly and honestly, in order to reduce the stigma and shame that surrounds it. Hungry to be Me by Julie Gauthier does exactly that. In this raw memoir Ms. Gauthier invites us to bear witness as she sifts through childhood memories and past relationships for clues about why this illness took hold of her and then persisted for decades. We share in her journey as she navigates the often confusing and sometimes painful path from decades of secret starvation to hospitalization to recovery. We can't help but cheer for her as she takes her life back, on her own terms, one heroic bite at a time. While she is finally able to embrace her whole self, imagined flaws and all, and allow space in her life for love, she cautions us that recovery from an eating disorder requires vigilance. Bravo Julie! As you have become your own hero, so too are you mine.

Vicki L. Nygaard
Professor of Sociology / Women's and Gender Studies
Vancouver Island, BC Canada

In her book, Julie gives us an honest testimonial about navigating mental health challenges and tacking the dichotomy of choice, when it comes to the desire to heal and make positive changes in one's life. Just like Julie, I believe that everyone has the capacity to make such changes. Specifically, by exploring the aspects of our lives that are not serving us well, we can start to shift how we orient ourselves in the world. In this sense, adopting a strength-based approach, where we assess what is working well in our lives, we can help solidify the changes we are working towards and become our own hero.

Dr. Anusha Kassan
Registered Psychologist, Associate Professor
The University of British Columbia

There is a singular magic that happens when a talented writer chooses to write their memoir with authenticity and vulnerability. Thankfully, Julie Gauthier has shared her story with us, taking us on a journey through childhood trauma and into her inner world, shadowed by her eating disorder. Despite years of secrecy and suffering, Julie's determination for healing and self-discovery is unshakeable; from the beginning, she bears the signature qualities of the hero she becomes. Julie's zest for life and connection to spirit are a refreshing reminder of the private victories we all share. Julie reminds us that the freedom to live our authentic nature is critical for our well-being and indeed, our survival. Her story is an inspiration for others and a reminder of the true costs when our social institutions continue to foster unattainable standards of beauty. We would do well to listen.

John de Freitas
Authenticity Coach | Author | Editor
Collaborative Author in *Daring to Share There to Here*

Absorbing parts of this impactful memoir often took me to my knees in tears of anguish, only to then lift me up to unimaginable heights of profound hope…over and over again. In addition to experiencing this uninterrupted cycle of human duality, I was taken aback at how many times Julie Gauthier's eloquent stories awakened me to damaged pieces of myself I didn't realize were broken and needed to be tended to. This is what a talented storyteller can accomplish when inspiration guides the deepest level of truth one is willing to share. Ms. Gauthier successfully achieves this feat by connecting the reader to her continuous desire to fight off her victim and welcome in her hero. As readers with unique stories of deception, including different settings, characters, and thoughts, Julie shares hers in a way that enables us to understand her mindset, connect to her emotions, and immerse ourselves in every struggle she bravely moves through. I instinctually found myself cheering for her and the reward of freedom she so justly deserves. Hungry to be Me describes the battle of a Heroine and Villain in a fairy tale, their equal fight for survival, along with the magical happy-ever-after of victory for all.

Diana Reyers
Author | Editor |Publisher
Founder of Daring to Share™ Global

In a devastatingly relatable fashion, Julie's memoir will hit every single chord of your heart and evoke every feeling possible. With tears in my eyes, I can't look away. Anger, grief, fear, guilt, joy. Those feelings all come to mind as I read. I urge everyone to open this book because once you do, you won't be able to put it down.

Sarah Lynn, Author
In Repair: From Existing to Living

There is so much I could write about Julie. Although, I met her only a few years ago and we didn't see each other very often, knowing her enriched my life. In Julie's presence I always felt totally free to say what I want, to laugh or cry when I want and to be myself without any judgement. I love and appreciate people like that because it allows me to be myself, to be a person with an energy of love, rather than fear, and therefore to be a better human being... and because it feels so good. I was lucky to experience Julie's Reiki healing and an Indian head massage—beyond this world—and I took Julie's yoga classes—a balm to my soul.

Julie's story touches me on so many levels. I never experienced an eating disorder, but I dealt with my own issues. I could see so many similarities in thinking and emotional processing. This is what I love about this book. The purpose of Julie's work goes beyond helping hundreds of people to deal with their own eating disorders, body image and self-value. It can also help people with all kinds of addiction, mental and emotional scars, and problems. It's the bravest thing to open up and share your own story but it's also the most effective in moving forward and healing yourself and others. Julie is making it happen. In her book Julie is sharing her healing journey with a raw honesty, and I am positive it will bring light and clarity to many lives.

I had a chance to photograph Julie twice. The first photo shoot was for her Reiki and Indian head massage branding. The second photo session was more personal. It was a boudoir—an intimate portrait, as I like to call it—session. This experience was all about fully accepting and celebrating her own body. I can't even describe the feelings I had while photographing Julie. When I saw the light falling on her skin, showing the lines and shapes of her body, I was amazed by the beauty. I will be forever grateful I had this opportunity, and I truly hope that these photographs helped Julie to see how extraordinary she is. I am a believer that the body and soul are inseparable, and the grace of the soul is a part of everyone's physical appearance.

I am very proud and happy for Julie for following her heart and choosing the less comfortable journey. This is what life is about. We have issues, mental and emotional blocks. We experience traumas and unfairness, and we are definitely not perfect. What matters is how we deal with it. Do we choose to search for our purpose, get up every day and be brave to define our issues, put a light on them and work step by step to grow and change for the better? It might be much harder but definitely worth it. I am so thankful I know a woman who is doing just that. Thank you, Julie, for everything you bring to this world.

Alice Sarog, Summer & Co. Photography

As a habit change coach, I know how strong the pull of old habits can be. Habits aren't just what we do daily, but they are also part of how we think and who we are. They have created neural pathways in the brain and become what is easiest and safest to do, not necessarily what is best to do. Changing our habits, our way of being, means re-wiring our brain. I hope you can see how difficult this can be and what Julie was up against. This is a beautifully written personal journey of fighting against who we believe ourselves to be through the stories we tell ourselves. Just like Julie, we are always telling ourselves stories and although they might feel like the truth, it doesn't mean that they are. It is not until we change our story that we can change our outcome.

Reading Julie's experience made me feel like I was my younger self sneaking around a friend's bedroom just to come across her journal which I could not help but read. It then made me feel what most of us would when uncovering someone's deepest darkest secrets and that is: disbelief. How could such a beautiful caring soul be struggling like this and why couldn't I see the signs? There is so much humanity in this story because all humans have three emotional needs: the need to be loved, the need to feel safe and the need to feel that we belong. It is hard to believe that such a hard fight could serve a purpose, but it was clear to me through reading her story that her eating disorder was actually helping her in fulfilling those needs. As hard as it may be to understand or even accept, every action has a positive intention, and I could see how her struggles were actually serving their purpose. It is not until she realized it for herself and how truly harmful this was to her physical health, emotional well-being and mental state that she made a decision that it was time to update the methods she used to receive love, safety and belonging.

Julie's vulnerability and honesty were not only a saviour for herself but will be for the many others who will read her story. You do not have to relate to the exact experience in order to relate to the emotions she felt. This story will help many. It takes an incredible amount of guts and courage to be so vulnerable in sharing the secrets so many of us continue to hide. However, it is only by sharing our truth that we inspire others to do the same. The truth really does set us free. She has accomplished what she has always wanted, by healing herself she now has the ability and capacity to help others. Julie is an incredibly compassionate human and by overcoming her own life challenges, she is now fully equipped to be the healer she always wanted to be. This is the best ending one could hope for. I know it was no small feat to get there but her story will give all those still struggling the glimmer of hope needed to push through. Thank you, Julie, for sharing your story with us.

Marie-Eve Ward
Habit Change Coach
@chitchatroomwithme

Gratitude

First and foremost, thank you to Helen No. In 2019, you were the Nurse Practitioner I confided in, and you took my case seriously from the start. You took me under your wing right away and started the process of helping me. I have no doubt that you are on the right career path as someone who listened to my history, believed in my story, and participated as actively as you could in my process towards recovery.

Secondly, the staff at the provincial adult tertiary eating disorders program at St-Paul's Hospital in Vancouver, each of you forever changed my life: from the kitchen staff to the laboratory technicians, doing daily blood work at 6:30 a.m. to the nurses with the patience of gold, the dieticians, the therapists, the social workers, psychologists, psychiatrists, and, last but not least, the Program Director of Research, Dr. Josie Geller; your immense amount of work ameliorates the program year after year.

Thank you to the Vista Residence and Discovery program in collaboration with Vancouver Coastal Health and all the health professionals who were supportive, caring, and available 24/7. Despite the pandemic and its challenges, you managed to provide online support during a six-month period before resuming residential treatment.

Thank you to Portia de Rossi for writing your book *Unbearable Lightness: A Story of Loss and Gain*—it gave me the clarity and hope I needed.

To John, soul brother and wonderful human being, thank you for your kindness, your unconditional support and for always meeting me where I am.

To Diana Reyers, for your patience, passion, compassion, and dedication, and for editing my words and story so beautifully to share and propel my message to the world. Thank you for trusting and inspiring me to be myself within my desire to throw poetry and imagery—the horse and the wolves—into a memoir! I feel immensely grateful to have met you.

Kay. Where to start! Thank you for always having my back, being my best cheerleader, encouraging me to pursue my dreams. Thank you for your patience and all the sacrifices you made to support me in writing this book. I have no words to convey the amount of love I have for you, and I feel blessed to walk this life by your side. Thank you for showing me what unconditional love is. I love you.

To my family and everyone who believed in me, supported me, and showed me the way to authenticity, so that I can live life to my full potential—freely and openly. Thank you.

And to you, the reader, thank you for being curious about my story and helping spread the message that recovery is certainly not linear but definitely possible.

Foreword

By Mélanie Fortin

I have had the privilege of knowing Julie for over thirty-two years—thirty-two years of friendship, complicity, and sharing many confidences. We were also roommates when we first left our family nest. So, I thought I profoundly knew her inside-out, convinced we had no secrets from one another. Therefore, when Julie asked me to write the foreword for her book, I immediately accepted because not only would it be an incredible project of collaboration with my best friend, but above all, it would be easy as a result of believing I knew everything about her...or so I thought.

As I began her book, I was stupefied to read a story I had no idea was so profoundly distressing—it was incredibly fragile yet so powerful at the same time. In fact, I realized I did not know her as well as I thought I did. To be frank, I was totally stunned and touched by her words.

This book is clearly in a class of its own; not because I have known Julie for so long, but because she presents authenticity in a way I have rarely seen in similar works. Julie purely, generously, and vulnerably gives herself to us without any filter or safety net. Along with the excellent quality of writing, this is one of the multiple reasons I was unable to stop as soon as I embarked on reading Julie's story. I have read thousands of books in my lifetime, and I can tell you without a doubt that this book will become a bestseller.

Since high school, Julie was nicknamed *the beautiful* due to her great natural beauty. She had everything needed to be successful and happy: elegance, charisma, intelligence, generosity, and talent in multiple areas. She shone with her presence and projected the image of a confident, happy, and accomplished woman. It is hard to believe that she hurt so much from within back then. Realizing it was just a facade, an armour for her to hide behind all those years really saddens me. However, I did know that she suffered deeply from a lack of self-confidence and that she clearly didn't see herself the way her friends and others perceived her. I remember her confiding in me many times that she didn't like her appearance and that she was unhappy with the way she looked or unsatisfied in relationships. Each time, I couldn't believe it. In my eyes and the eyes of everyone, she had everything necessary to be happy; this is the problem with a mental illness like eating disorders—it cannot be seen by the naked eye.

I got to know Julie a few months after her ski accident. Who would have thought that her eating disorders started at that moment? Through all these years, when she didn't think she was beautiful or thought she was *too fat* or did not trust herself, I remember telling her she was worrying for *nothing* and totally minimizing her actual feelings. Not for a second did I have any idea that her relationship with food was already so problematic. Clearly, her discomfort was much deeper, more insidious, and most of all, it was destroying her by taking up all the space within her.

Julie wears her heart on her sleeve. She gives without keeping score—so much that she tends to forget about herself. I used to call her Mother Teresa! She never prioritized herself… until 2019. The day she told me she was considering going to an eating disorder center was when I realized her great inner suffering, and yet, I could still not fully comprehend the extent of the emotional turmoil she was going through.

In this enlightening book, Julie reveals passages from her diary, sharing how she experienced this ordeal from the inside. She makes us realize how much eating disorders are present in the world and how much damage they can do, including death. Reading her memoir not only educated me but helped me understand more about the intricacies of eating disorders, a subject I knew only a little bit about. She reiterates how unfortunate it is that disordered eating is not discussed enough in a society where it is more prevalent now than ever before.

At forty-five years old, Julie chose herself. Through this book, she reveals a descent into hell and a stunning comeback due to her arduous but determined quest for happiness through a powerful awakening where she finally becomes the hero of her own life.

Through a deep exercise of humility and truth, the *real Julie* reveals her most inspiring journey. It will give wings to all those who live with similar problems and the strength to go within to find their own way.

Julie, my best friend, thank you for being you.
I am proud of you. I love you xxx. Mélanie

Introduction

Hello, and thank you for picking up this book.

I know there are many wonderful stories out there focused on inspiring and supporting women, and I am truly humbled that you decided to read my memoir, so I can share the message I have wanted to communicate for so long.

My 33-year battle with eating disorders is unfortunately not an isolated case. It was a challenge for me to put my story on paper and send it out into the world, even though I knew my message was important to share. As I wrote, my inner critic spoke loudly in my ear, asking me questions like: *Who do you think you are? Do you really think you are so special that you had to write a book about your suffering?* When I reflected on this, the obvious answer was that I am not unique. And yet, unfortunately, my story is also not unique. So, with more than one million Canadians suffering from eating disorders and disordered eating, I concluded that it was my responsibility to do my part to support others struggling with an illness that continues to catch her prey at a younger and younger age.

If someone had told me three years ago that I would be in recovery now, I would not have believed them. Throughout my journey, the numerous stories of unworthiness I told myself were displaced with signs and symptoms of my eating disorders. I was good at it—very good. But at one pivotal point, I knew I had to make a change because, bit by bit, I was dying from the inside. Things began to change when I asked for help.

Everyone who endures their specific hurting battles suffers through their own unique story. To be clear, my story is not intended to be compared with anyone else's because one person's narrative is not more or less relevant than someone else's. The intention behind this book is very simple: I want to share my story so others can partake in doing the same without shame. Everyone needs to speak their truth, so we all shine our light while becoming our own heroes.

Within my writings, you will absorb passages of my journal and explore the reflections I experienced through my process of pre-hospitalization and rehabilitation towards recovery. This book was written for anyone who wants an honest perspective on what someone with an eating disorder can go through, emotionally, physically and mentally. I am very transparent about what thoughts went through my distressed mind and what the path to recovery felt like, including the dichotomy of choice I worked through within my decision to recover. As much as I experienced a great deal of agony moving through my treatment, I wanted to publish this book to reiterate that there is hope within the subsequent victory of becoming your hero. The pain does lessen for all involved—the sufferer and those close to them.

I see you. And I want you to believe that, even though recovery might not be linear, it is possible. And even though recovery might not be easy, it is achievable.

So many of us go through life with our stories hidden, feeling ashamed or afraid when our whole truth doesn't live up to some established ideal...
That is until someone dares to start telling that story differently.

~Michelle Obama

What I hope for is that each of us freely tells our story, so we all live in authenticity.

With love and gratitude, Julie

Hungry to be Me

Hungry to Belong

Journal Entry
October 10, 2019

I just meditated for a little more than 20 minutes. My brain could not shut down. I'm greatly overwhelmed. I have so much to do with so little time to do it all. I don't know where to start. When I am nervous and anxious to that extent, I freeze without being able to get anything done. I find myself numbing by either scrolling away on social media or shutting it all down by sleeping 15 hours a day. Mind you, I am exhausted. But when my mind gets this busy, I can't seem to handle stress very well, and I always end up here, in this state of chaos.

I'm so confused. I feel my stomach growling so early at the beginning of the day, and I'm at a loss of what to do. My body image struggles are off the charts while I debate if I should eat or not. Physically, I am hungry, but my eating disorder's mind tells me I shouldn't get anything to eat if I want to reach what I think are my ideal body weight and shape goals. I know what the right thing to do is, but at the same time, I can't seem to agree with myself. I delay the inevitable and wonder if I should resort to having a coffee first. I have been obsessed with coffee for the past week. Is it because I know I have to abstain from caffeine for seven weeks from the time I enter treatment? I've already been told that I won't be able to have as much coffee when I'm hospitalized. I am currently trying to limit my intake because, with everything else I will be going through, the torture of withdrawing from caffeine is the last thing I need. Maybe I am sensing a loss of control and feeling paralyzed because I am actually taking control of my life by going to treatment, but I won't be able to control what happens once I am there. I think this is what scares me, along with my eating disorders. And yet, I am excited to leave for treatment soon. My mind goes back to the coffee—the less I want to think about it, the more it takes over my thoughts. It's been one of my best friends for so long.

Realistically, my to-do list is not that long. I have a few more yoga classes to teach at the studio, a one-day women's retreat to facilitate on the twentieth, and I need to pack my bags for my stay in Vancouver. It's just that my plate feels so much fuller. Heading to Vancouver on October 28th, I will be sleeping in a hotel close to the hospital downtown as my admission date is the next morning at nine. My eating disorder mind wants to engage in symptoms so badly. In fact, it wishes I could immerse myself fully into them before being admitted because I know that once I am there, I won't be able to. And that scares the shit out of me. So, I want to restrict and fast, and juice, and lose as much weight as I can before I get there, but my obsession pushes me to act the exact opposite way, eating like there is no tomorrow. I have landed in guilt, judgment and shame.

Yesterday after I finished teaching my class at the studio, someone asked me if I was pregnant. It wasn't the first time, but I had not heard this since quitting the airline a year ago, so it took me off guard and immediately brought me back to a place of worthlessness. I become hyper-focused on why I repeatedly get asked that question.

I try to snap out of it, but when my mind gets too quiet, it goes back to that place of inadequacy.

When I got the call telling me that I was now number one on the list for treatment at Saint Paul's Hospital, I ate like it was my last meal, my last day on this earth—I ate all day, and every day since feels the exact same way. I guess, for me to dissociate from everything that I like and hate about myself, I just couldn't stop eating. I was numbing. Numbing. Numbing. It was like I was figuratively on death row, awaiting execution, and all parts of me were about to die. It honestly felt like I was going to cease to exist. I know a part of me will experience grief from losing the "old Julie" in order to make space for the "new Julie," the one who wants to be freed from what she experienced in the past and that she is still experiencing. My wish is that one day I can shine, but at the same time, I am afraid to be perceived as pretentious if I welcome the self-love and self-confidence I, logically, know I deserve—that we all deserve.

It's so strange that I wish self-love for others but can't seem to commit to it myself. I want my yoga students to feel welcomed, seen, heard, and respected; to feel accepted and loved, yet, I have the most difficult time reflecting that love towards myself. Sometimes, I think I don't matter, making spreading love to others my mission and purpose so I don't have to worry about what I need. At the same time, I remember someone asking me: "How can we live on an empty tank?" "It fuels me to do so," I responded. What she said next kind of slapped me in the face: "Maybe you dig deep in losing yourself through teaching and healing others, avoiding finding that love for yourself; it's not sustainable." Despite knowing she was right, I didn't want to admit it at the time. I had lost myself deeper in creating loving relations outside myself.

Since opening up to others about my mental illness, I have come across many women who suffer from eating disorders or disordered eating in general; it is a real affliction. Most people I encounter suffer from either bulimia or anorexia nervosa. Their stories are so heartbreaking to hear, and with most of them you could never tell they have the illness. I do not know any men suffering from this disease, but I know they exist. The fact that my story is not that uncommon makes me feel uncomfortable. It's not that I needed or wanted to be "so special," but it feels strange because I was isolated for so long. It also feels like I am making a considerable fuss telling the world about something they already know about. The inner critic presents fully, asking me, "Do you really think you are so special? Are you really sick enough to go to treatment?" She finishes off with the final cutting statement: "You are such an attention-seeker!" The accumulation of all this takes me to heightened feelings of shame and guilt. Again. What a fucked-up thing!

Seeing others "succeed" at their ED makes me feel I have failed at mine. It actually sounds irrational that there could be such a thing as failing at a mental illness. But in my head, yeah, there is such a thing. In the jargon of the subject, the type of eating disorder I suffer from is "binge-eating disorder." That very term makes me feel disgusting and repulsive. The very image I have in my mind about my disorder is as gross as the reflection I see in the mirror.

Like many others who suffer from this sneaky disease, I once reopened the garbage can to take back what I threw away. I initially put the item in the bin to eliminate the temptation of eating it. I started not wanting the food because I wanted to avoid it, but then got obsessed about it and found myself retrieving it from the garbage. To say I am not proud about this is an understatement, but the saddest thing is that I am not alone. I was told by many others that they also succumbed to this U-turn. As weird as it seems, there is a strange feeling of relief, knowing that others go through similar behaviours. It also affects my ego with its voice at a high volume, telling me how pathetic I am. This becomes the start of my pity party, and I wonder where that attitude comes from. I never felt that way before. I am so low and depressed with what seems to be an empty soul and nothing left to offer—nothing at all. I am so done with this.

I'm done hating myself, done body checking myself, criticizing myself and disliking what I see in the mirror. Like what the actual fuck! Multiple times I was tempted to "drop it" and be part of the statistics of those who succumbed to the disease. I couldn't give two fucks about life anymore. But now, I am really looking forward to giving it a shot by going to treatment. I do not want to be part of the eating disorders' statistics anymore.

Exhaustion has taken over my life, and I can't wait to do absolutely nothing, to have nothing to think about, nothing to do except work on my healing and take care of my health. And sleep. I am certain it will be both a benefit and a relief to do less, and I can feel excitement stirring up inside me. I like to joke that my bags are now packed and ready at the door. October 29th cannot come fast enough. I have waited all my life for this moment. Each passing day led me here, and I am so grateful.

I have such a great support system around me, and I'm looking forward to planning my new life when I return home from the hospital. I wonder if I will be totally healed or if I will still have the eating disorder mind once I complete treatment. I am aiming for full recovery. My best friend, Mélanie, told me not to put too much hope in that final result, but I do anyway. I know she is not coming from a bad place as she only wants me to be happy and to finally find the peace and happiness I am looking for. However, as a neuro-linguistic coach, she thinks seven weeks is a short time to fully change behaviours that have been there for so long. But I am so hopeful. I WANT to be hopeful. The only thing I have is hope. I am hopeful, and I am certain 2020 will be one of the best years. Yes, it will be MY YEAR, an exceptional year of healing and moving forward.

I can't wait to be healed and help others. I don't want any other human being to hate themselves the way I do. I don't wish this on anyone.

I often wonder what happened to her, the younger me. Where is that beautiful soul that was once a shining child? Where did it all start?

It's January 10, 1987, and I am shivering. The snow on the back of my neck sneakily makes its way in between my scarf and winter jacket with cold claws moving up to the front of my throat. They press me deeper into the ground before invading my face, and ultimately, reaching every part of my body from the crown of my head to my fingertips and toes. My entire being is paralyzed, yet a slight ripple sensation of floating comes over me. Although my physical body is trapped, it seems that my mind is floating on waves of thoughts that take place between resilience and apprehension, peace and fear, and between letting go and holding on to what is happening to me. Suddenly, a trail of questions come over me: *Why can't I warm up? Why can't I move? Am I paralyzed? How am I going to get out of this?*

I become very clear that I want this freezing, raw, piercing sensation to go away.

I can't even open my eyes to witness where I am. All I see is darkness, and I am acutely conscious of the silence surrounding me; if there is any noise within my radius, I cannot hear it.

Where am I? The environment feels so foreign to me within the confusion of my senses. My mind moves in all directions, North, South, East and West, but my body remains unresponsive despite my efforts. Inert, I am one with the landscape, like a contemporary piece of art inaugurated in the middle of nowhere, so abstract and out of context that it almost belongs there. Not easy to notice, yet subtly captured by the eye from afar.

Suddenly, it hits me—this must be a dream! Yes, that is it, I must be dreaming! I'm having a nightmare, desperately trying to wake up from it. *You can do this,* I repeat over and over again, reassuring my tormented twelve-year-old self. Wake up, Julie; this is only a nightmare. I try to convince myself one last time before finally giving up, exhausted from the demanding energy required to fight the sensation of a thousand sharp knives stabbing my body in an attempt to warm itself up. This is agonizing, and my confused brain can't handle it anymore. I find myself allowing survival mode to kick in, succumbing to my physical body drowning into unconsciousness.

*My mind is no longer able to swim the waves of
peace and resilience.
So, I let go and allow the natural state of survival to take me
to the ambiguity of the unknown.*

I am now lying in a comatose state on this cold white bed of snow, holding me tight as if tucked into bed for a long night's sleep. It is time to wait until someone notices me from a distance.

A few days later, I woke up in the hospital. I am told that I hit a tree while alpine skiing.

I'm asked if I remember anything about the accident. No. All I recollect is that I wanted to wake up from that nightmare. Do I recall how long I laid there before anyone noticed me? I do not. But I am sure that I had an angel watching over me because I was found with little time left before perishing into the forest; half an hour later, and I would not be alive today.

I also don't remember much from the first six months to a year after waking up from the craniotomy that further saved my life and any long-term damage. A hole was drilled into my skull over the subdural hematoma area that developed, and the build-up of blood was suctioned out through the hole. There are very few significant moments here and there that I vaguely remember.

I found out later from my father that he held my hand before going into the operating room. Apparently, I was experiencing convulsions, and I was debating with the hospital staff. With his gentle voice, my father reassured me: *It's okay, Julie, I am here, and everything will go well.* The surgery lasted two hours. He told me he was in the waiting room and cried like he never cried before, praying to whoever would hear him to save me. It breaks my heart to think about him, alone in the waiting room for two hours, praying and crying for his child to survive. I do not have kids, so I can't relate, but I know how much I love my dad, and I would never want him to be in such distress.

During the first four days, I slept, unaware of what was going on. Apparently, my mother attempted to take my hand to caress it, but even a slight, gentle touch hurt me; every cell of my body was in pain. All she did was sit by my bedside, watching me sleep and heal as there was nothing else for her to do but be there for me.

I remember that my mother wanted me to drink because I was dehydrated, but I wasn't thirsty. I was tired, and everything seemed like so much of a struggle and an extra effort. However, I was prepared to drink or eat anything to heal faster, and I remember the plastic trays the hospital food was served on. My morning peanut butter toast was soaked with humidity every morning, but I was grateful and didn't make a fuss about it. I was never a picky eater, consuming almost everything on my plate; I was a gourmand young child with a great appreciation for food. In this case, I mostly wanted to eat anything to improve faster.

A week or so after the surgery, I stood up with my mother's help, and asked to look at myself in the mirror. My mother told me that half of my head was shaved, so I was curious to see what I looked like. I was fascinated that they used a razor to shave my head for the operation. I have often wondered what this process entailed; in what manner did they approach removing the hair from my fragile skull? Was it done in a conscious, precautious, delicate, mindful way? Or was it more automatic and fast paced? I know that time was of the essence to remove the blood from my skull, so the manner in which my hair was removed didn't really matter. But, interestingly enough, the inner child in me always wanted to know. To this day, I would still love to see how they did it from a bird's eye view.

Standing with my mother in front of that hospital mirror for the first time after my surgery, I couldn't believe it was me. I didn't recognize myself with the white of my left eyeball metamorphosed to the most vivid red I had ever seen. There was such a contrast with the right eyeball being as white as the snow I skied on the day of my accident. I knew it was the left side of my head that they shaved, but when I saw the result, I felt a swell of emotion slowly building in me. I, simultaneously, felt compassion for myself, as well as deep mourning for who I once was.

My reflection was similar to the cubist Picasso painting, *Girl before a Mirror*: asymmetric, colourful, and intense with the addition of my mother's reflection standing behind me, waiting for any reaction I would have. My image resembled an oil on canvas of a young girl lost in her own eyes with her mother worrying about what emotions would come next. I saw a grotesque reflection of various shapes and dark colours of mostly reds. There was the brilliant red in her eye where the white used to glow. Her hair was asymmetrical, and there was a scar where stitches displayed the reality and absurdness of this moment she was absorbed in. I feel this painting that I have never seen before was dedicated to me, with its beauty initially being perceived and classified as marginally different.

Even though I was drawn to the uniqueness of my image, I decided to shave the rest of my head, so it appeared symmetrical. For some reason, I also thought it might help me heal faster. I have never really thought about or realized that my naive twelve-year-old self was a fighter at a very young age, ready to do anything to rehabilitate faster. And so, my fight began as I delved into the recovery of the effects of my accident.

It turns out that this would not be the last time
I fought for healing in my life in one way or another.

One of the most memorable events during my rehabilitation was when I first tried to talk, and nothing came out from my mouth the way I wanted it to. My speech was greatly affected, but it was also luckily quickly recovered. My memory was also altered, and I didn't remember how to write anymore. When I decided to start writing, I came up blank and burst into tears, grasping the pencil while wondering how to spell the words. It was puzzling as the letters didn't easily leave their trace on the paper like they used to. I used wrong letters in place of others, and in some cases, the letters were reversed or upside down. It was like I knew the dance choreography in my head, but I couldn't physically put the dance steps together to make sense of them. I felt empty with so many unanswered questions:

How long will this take? How will I be able to do this? Will I be able to go back to school and be with my friends? I had a haggard look about me, understanding that everything I learned in my short life was taken away. Not only was my pre-developed level of academic skills significantly reduced, but I also lost my freedom and independence, as well as my 12-year-old pride. This was probably one of the hardest parts of my rehabilitation. Although my academic skills slowly returned, it is evident to me now that I experienced some unhealed emotional trauma for years to come.

Another very vivid recollection of my post-surgery-stay at the hospital is having the thought that my mother was not coming to see me on one particular day. I became accustomed to her arriving at my bedside at six o'clock every morning. Even if all she did was watch me sleep and heal, when she still had not arrived by six-thirty when I woke up, I felt so lost and alone without her by my side. Arriving a little bit later at around 6:30 a.m., I was so relieved she had finally made it. She explained that she was late because she got stuck in traffic. I remember feeling abandoned without understanding why. I now appreciate the love I felt from my mother caring for me during that time. She provided me with the emotional safety I needed that carried me through my stay at the hospital. I subconsciously knew she was coming every morning, supporting me with an emotional soft and warm safety blanket.

If that blanket had a colour, it would be pale blue. It would contrast with the pale green walls of the semi-private hospital room I had. I had a neighbour in that room, but I never met him. My mother told me that another kid on the same hospital floor had a basketball accident who hit his head on the gymnasium floor. She walked me around in a wheelchair to the different floors, and I wanted to make friends. I have always been a very social child, but, although around so many patients in the hospital, I felt isolated with no one my age I could relate to or exchange similar experiences with. I felt that, despite all the good intentions, nobody really understood what I was going through—I would have liked to talk with someone who had a head injury as well.

I find a child's thought processes so interesting as they develop patterns and behaviours of survival based on the stories they tell themselves. The day that my mother arrived late created a broken pattern of safety that left a mark on me. Since that time, I don't think I have ever been as relieved to see my mother as when she showed up at the door of my hospital room that day. She entered my room, breathless from hurrying to get to me before I awoke; I remember her face with her dark brown hair framing her wide open big blue eyes. The feeling of being extremely distraught to then experiencing heightened relief made an incredible impact on me that I carried with me into adulthood. As I relive those moments, I am intrigued with how the brain of a child functions to survive emotionally.

During the thirty minutes I waited for her, an entire scenario happened in my head, one where I believed she wasn't coming and forgot me. Again. When I recognized the pattern of her coming to me every morning, I felt like this was it—I was getting my mother back! I felt that this time, the bond I was looking for with her was real and here to stay. Because of different past situations and events, like my parents having twins when I was three years old, I had a sense…a feeling…a story in my head that I wasn't enough for my mother and that she was never really proud of me or even wanted a connection with me. Despite believing I was trying to connect with her, it didn't seem to work in my favour because I wasn't getting the feedback I was looking for. However, in the hospital, I received the feedback I was seeking steadily for a week. It was happening. She came every morning for several days in a row. Then, she suddenly broke the pattern because of the slow traffic. The story I made up in my mind was that I was now worthy of my mother because she came to see me every day—it felt like my wishes and hopes had finally come true. But then, my mother got stuck in traffic that day, and because I felt vulnerable and depended on her 6:00 a.m. arrival, I created a different story that included being abandoned when she arrived late.

I carried that story and others that evolved from it with me for many years, and they shaped the way I responded to the world throughout my life. I still sometimes make up stories in my head, but I now have the tools to catch myself doing it when I am in that space; I'm now able to clarify what is real for me and what is not. But as a kid, I didn't have the self-awareness or capacity to perception-check or express myself.

Apparently, two weeks after my surgery, I left the hospital with my mother. She recently told me that I had a huge smile on my face and a scarf on my head, preventing me from getting cold, but I don't remember. It's a significant piece of my childhood that I recall very little of. I have no memory of leaving a place where I spent the most critical time of my life. Because it was. It was a period of time that changed me forever, and I wish I could remember the freedom of leaving the hospital as I headed to my house to reunite with my father and my siblings, who are three years younger than me.

A few days after I arrived at our family home, my parents and I decided that I would not go back to high school. I had so much to recover, and we realized it would have been too difficult to achieve the same level of learning the other children had reached while relearning all I had lost. It was also wintertime, and I had issues with my equilibrium, so my parents were not comfortable having me walk to school in case I fell and hit my head again. They hired a tutor for a few weeks, but I became exhausted quickly, so we decided to cancel the sessions. It was disappointing not to go back to school, but at the same time, I was not certain I wanted to show up with no hair and a scar on my head. A few of my friends came to see me during my recovery, but I lost many as time went on, and I felt very left out and lonesome. I started to sleep a lot.

Not only was I exhausted with the intellectual work I had to do, but my mental health took a real toll. I wore headbands and bandanas and felt miserable. I did not know how to be cool within my situation—I could not be cool. Strangers bullied me, making fun of my scarves and judging me, not knowing why I was wearing them. It was hurtful. I still have pictures of me during that time, and they are genuinely not my favourites!

Feeling unseen for what I was going through, all I wanted to do was sleep all day. I began fighting hunger and it brought me a lot of comfort through self-soothing. I recognized something was off because I didn't feel the joy I thought I was supposed to be experiencing as a 12-year-old. It was easy for me to blame being tired as an excuse for not having dinner. It was all true, I didn't feel well, I was tired, I had stomach aches and headaches, but I was manipulating the information for my own sake to not eat. I was depressed. I had no idea at the time, but I can now see how sneaky the eating disorder presented itself into my life. One day at the time, it crept in and took over.

My parents and I never really talked about my accident after being deemed physically healed and, what appeared to be, mentally healed. I had a few visits to a psychologist, but at the time, I refused further treatment because I knew it was pricey, and I felt guilty that my parents were paying a lot of money for me to talk to an adult. The few times I went, I remember the therapist wanting me to express my feelings. She asked me to scream to vent the anger she thought or wanted me to have. I didn't know how to, and I didn't understand the concept at the time. I thought it was ridiculous.

When I decided to write my story, I wanted to discuss my accident with my parents. I realized that I never had the chance to find out what happened, how they felt, and how they interpreted me moving out of my depression while sneakily trading it for my eating disorder.

After talking with my mother and father, they tearfully expressed how traumatic the experience was for them too, which I never really thought about beforehand. Listening to them was very emotional for me but also very beautiful. I am now at an age whereby I can understand and somewhat empathize with the pain a parent experiences when on the verge of losing a child. Having never had a child, I will never fully understand the extent of that feeling, but when I saw the redness and tears in my father's eyes when we Skyped about the past, I felt his hurt despite the physical distance between us. I witnessed his torment without being able to hold him and show him that I am here for him just as he was there for me so many years ago.

After being discharged from my second treatment for eating disorders in August 2020, I had a revelation. I was visiting my hometown of Montreal, and my mother who lives in Africa was there as well because of the Covid Pandemic. We met and talked. I asked if she would be comfortable sharing details about what she remembered about my accident. She shared a memory that surfaced when she learned I was admitted to treatment. She told me that when I was in the hospital, I had issues with my equilibrium and couldn't bathe myself for fear that I might fall and hit my head again.

So, she helped bathe me,
and while removing my hospital gown from my fragile,
traumatized body, I looked at myself and thrillingly said:
"Wow, look, mom, I lost weight!"

I do not remember that pivotal moment. However, reflecting back, it makes so much sense because I was always looking for her approval. I wanted her to be proud of me for losing weight. Among other things, she used diets and exercise to appear younger and thinner, so I thought she would be pleased. My mother didn't make a big deal about me talking about my weight or that I lost weight because her mind was on other things. She was rightfully absorbed in the trauma of almost losing her oldest child while, simultaneously, managing a household and a deficient marriage. With my 46-year-old lens, and despite her disregarding my victorious comment, I recognize that I was way too happy that I lost weight and wanted to impress her. I was also disappointed that she didn't celebrate with me. The story I wanted my mother to hear was that with barely any effort, I succeeded at something she worked hard at—all it took was a ski accident and two weeks in intensive care.

This was the precise moment my eating disorder took my freedom away from me, like a pack of hungry wolves finding and surrounding their prey not allowing me to escape.

Hungry to Heal

Journal Entry
October 14, 2019

With less than two weeks before I go to treatment, I start to feel the resistance and the dichotomy of my choices, the separation between my rational and disordered mind. My irrational mind wants me to cancel the treatment. I have doubts about it all, and I want to abandon the whole thing. I have reflected on it and concluded there isn't any treatment that will help me recover from what I am experiencing anyways. Until yesterday, I was hopeful, but now I think it was pretty naive on my part to think it might work. I really think that since I had nothing else to cling to, I settled on the idea that treatment would save me, the thought that I would have something to look forward to, day after day. I believed I could have something to sustain me, support me every day, and help me paint the picture of what could be a future I didn't see myself. But honestly, who am I kidding?

I seem to have forgotten the excitement I was raving about a few days ago. I have totally pushed memories of hope and positivism so far back that I can't even remember the fact they ever existed. Where is that hope I felt, so tangible I could almost taste it? I had so much hope.

My mind goes back and forth to the pros and cons of going to Vancouver; I am negotiating with myself. The fact that I can heal in seven weeks is pretty slim anyways—Mélanie was right, telling me not to focus on the end result of such a short time frame. On top of that, I have other worries starting to bubble up. I am worried financially, not working for a minimum of a month and a half. I also do not know if I will need additional residential treatment afterwards; this could add 15 weeks to the equation. That means I won't be working for a total of four months with monthly rent still to pay and no savings at the bank.

I still have the same body image issues, not liking what I see in the mirror. I am not going to the gym or yoga as much as I would like. I am physically and emotionally drained, but at the same time, a part of me tells me I am lazy, and that is why I am not in the shape I want to be in and "should" be in. My eating disorder mind convinces me that this is why I am not reaching my goals; I am not dedicated enough. However, every muscle in my body aches and my breathing is shortened very easily. Just a little bit of physical activity like climbing the stairs makes me feel breathless. So, I try to go to gentle yoga classes. It feels so great to be in the studio.

I continue to feel like I am eating too much, even though I don't know what eating too much means anymore. I have lost many landmarks. I don't know what is good, what is not good, what is less, what is too much.

Journal Entry
October 21, 2019

Eight days. I am feeling more balanced and grounded today.

I hesitated to do so, but I decided to call my father and explain what was going on with my life and my health and what I am going to get treatment for. At first, I wasn't sure if I wanted to tell my family, except my sister—she has known what is going on for a long time. However, I didn't know how to approach my parents about this. I didn't want them to be sad or in distress. I didn't want them to make a big deal about it; I am not looking for pity, quite the opposite, actually. But I finally decided to tell them because if the roles were reversed, I would like to know if either of them had a health condition, especially since we all live in different provinces and countries.

My father always kind of knew I had unexplained feelings of constantly looking for "more" and feeling incomplete. As a young adult, I always felt something was missing in me and that I was marginalized, never feeling satisfied with any of the life situations I ended up in.

When I was in my 30s, after I moved from Quebec to British Columbia, I confided in him that I didn't know what I was looking for in life and that I believed to a certain degree that my mission to find the secret to that sparkle of joy seemed doomed.

This is probably one of the reasons I moved so many times in my life. I moved more than 22 times in less than 10 years. I always get excited about my next move and then become blasé about it; it's like I discover that what I was looking for ended up not being there. I made it a mission to keep moving until I reached that sense of belonging, that deep feeling I have always been looking for.

Yeah, the search can be long and hard when you don't even know what you are looking for! I hung onto this feeling that I would "know" when it showed up in front of me, but this now feels utopian and unsustainable—it's exhausting. To be candid, when it came to choosing where I lived, I always followed my gut, my intuition, and this is one of the reasons I ended up in British Columbia, at the other end of the country from where I was born.

There was nothing more painful than listening to my dad cry on the phone when I told him about my eating disorder. It was unbearable to hear or even have the slightest knowledge that his heart was hurting. But, in the end, I feel relieved that I told him. I also emailed my mother about it, and she is very supportive of the process.

Journal Entry
October 28, 2019

I am in Vancouver, heading to the hospital tomorrow morning to start my seven-week stay. I am now really excited and back to being enthusiastic and confident about the process because I desire to be hopeful through this journey. I do not want to have any more doubts whatsoever about going. I am ready for this journey, and I will do everything in my power to succeed.

In May 2019, a few months before I was admitted to my first treatment at St-Paul's hospital, I had a vision during a meditation. I was brought back to my 1987 ski accident scene, and I had never experienced this before. Outside of this particular time, lying in a place of stillness on my mat and after all these years, I never fully remembered or had any flashbacks of the accident.

In my meditation, it is a clear sunny day with no clouds in the sky, exactly like the day of my accident. It seems that I am walking on the top of a mountain. I am content, and as I look around, my lips gently form a smile. There is an aura of quiet and calm as I breathe in the fresh air and feel the cool weather on my skin; everything is vivid and very realistic. I admire the beautiful pure white snow on the trees as the splendid blue sky and the sun simultaneously show off their magnificent and warm rays of light. I am at peace. Then, I see someone lying on the snow a few meters from me. It doesn't take me long to realize it is me, 32 years earlier. Within my meditation, I am an outsider of my accident scene, seeing my younger self lying in the snow, wearing a yellow winter jacket and white mittens. My short blond hair is floating on what seems to be cold cotton candy. There is no trace of blood, and I look serene with my eyes closed. Suddenly, I see the soul, her soul—my soul, leaving her young body. She died from her accident. As her soul runs to fly up towards the skies, a beautiful angel stops its momentum and asks the soul: *What are you doing, where are you going?* It answers: *I am leaving; she is dead; it's time to find another body. But the angel is relentless: You can't leave her like this. Look at her. She is still so young, with so much to accomplish and a life to live; her time is not over yet.* Both the angel and the soul looked over towards the body lying on the ground. The soul repeats itself: *But she is…* The angel disagrees with the soul and interrupts and becomes more assertive. She says: *Go back. She is not done. She needs to live her life's purpose.*

I then saw her soul,
my soul, going back towards the dormant body,
melting down into the yellow of my jacket
the same way it came out of it,
bringing life back to the young girl,
so, she could continue living her life—my life.

I find it very interesting that this vision appeared at this specific moment in my life when I was ready to heal and seek the reasons why I hid in my eating disorders for so many years. I desperately wanted to finally find the freedom that was taken away from me so long ago. I always felt the uncomfortable sensation created while living somewhat incongruent with my true self; there was a feeling that something didn't align with me and my values. I knew that I needed to uncover and shift something, but I didn't know what I was looking for. I wanted to be real, genuine, authentic, and show up as truthful, but I was unconsciously acting in a way I thought people wanted me to be. I was a people-pleaser, often hiding my insecurities and rejecting potential friendships and relationships in fear that I would, in turn, be rejected if I committed to them. So, instead of moving through this painful process, I would just fast forward to the latter and reject myself first by hiding within destructive behaviors. This way of being actually served me at the time, allowing me to displace discomfort instead of dealing with the uneasiness that comes with it. Being preoccupied with my weight and the reflection of my image in the mirror has always been a way for me to escape and withdraw from what I need to pay attention to. My pursuit of chasing perfection was a vicious cycle, keeping the business at hand in my head while re-validating my unworthiness. It was, and still sometimes is, such a strong force within me that doesn't go away. Again, there was such a separation between who I was and the authentic person I wanted to be, and I couldn't escape the thoughts of wanting to be someone else. I didn't want to be me.

When I read the journal entries from 2019, I now realize how I indeed lost myself greatly within the loving relations I created outside myself. Not only that, but I also lost myself in non-loving relationships that allowed people to treat me poorly, just as I treated myself. Most of my romantic relationships have been with men who could not value me and what I had to offer them. All my past partners told me in one way or another that I had to lose weight if I wanted to be more attractive—for them to actually desire me. Another one bought me fat burners on our second date because he knew I was starting to compete in bodybuilding, and he wanted to *help* me get leaner faster. He later admitted that he wanted to be with me because he saw the physical potential I had, probably thinking that I would be more slender and toned within a few months of working out hard enough. Another one admitted that his friends told him I was too pretty to be with him, and the only reason he could possibly be in my *league* was that I was overweight. Men never had any problem offering to sleep with me, but they always had something to say about my physique once we were in a relationship. I recognize that tolerating that kind of behaviour from someone who says they love me is a sign of low self-esteem and simultaneously a sign of being emotionally and mentally abused. I have learned and I no longer endure those kinds of comments, knowing how loving and caring relationships should be—or how I now want them to be. I am also conscious that I am the only one responsible for allowing each of these men to devalue me. They were on their own journey of suffering and healing, and we were not aligned to heal together at that time. They have been great teachers, and I wouldn't be the person I am today if I had not jumped through those relationship hurdles. With some hindsight, I am positive that I unconsciously sought out relationships with no chance of working. I did this to spare myself going through disappointment, hurt, and heartbreak. There was no recipe for success within these relationships where lack of trust, doubt, and miscommunication were part of the blend.

I sought trust, love, empathy, compassion, and meaningful connections, and yet, I couldn't offer the same to the person who was the most important in my life—me. No wonder I felt my relationships, and not only the romantic ones, felt disingenuous, even though I was striving for the exact opposite. Deep down, I wanted all my relationships to be genuine, but there was always this non-spoken, undeniable truth that I wasn't able to reach out for. I looked everywhere for it—or so I thought.

I am a truth seeker, and always have been. I have constantly and continuously been curious about discovering and exploring who I am to the fullest extent. My mission continued to be finding that lost joy. But I also had parts of me that wanted to give up because the suffering deep inside me was too great. In my pursuit of seeking happiness as a place or destination, I moved so many times in my life while ignoring being in the appreciation of the moment. Before I went into treatment, I could count on my hands the moments I was fully conscious of being authentically happy. One time when I was a flight attendant, I remember a colleague asked me if I was happy during a night flight. This made me heavyhearted because I knew the answer was negative. Still, I appeared to have it all: a fantastic job travelling the world, a condo, living in a beautiful city and country, and my health. Having an eating disorder is not the healthiest one can be, but I was still able to work, do sports and live a somewhat privileged situation. However, that empty feeling I could never voice was always inside me. I continued to question when it began.

Recently, for the first time in my life, after practicing yoga and lying in Shavasana, I was able to talk to my inner child. It wasn't one hundred percent effective because, as much as I tried to connect with her, she was blurry, and I couldn't make her appear in front of me—she also had difficulty seeing me. I am not even sure if she knows who I am. I wonder what that means. I wonder if this carries some sort of significance.

Let me show you the way to the unknown rules of
my mind, thoughts, and life.
Let me show you the road that no one knew about.
Let me show you the hidden path I hid for so long.
The expansion or road trip—unplanned—left me with
no other choice
to vocalize my need for direction and guidance.
Today, I wish I could show you the way to a better love,
a better life, and a joyful you.

~ Julie Gauthier

I think back to my ski accident recovery when mental health took the reins without me noticing, and when I decided how I was supposed to look. I really am certain that was the coping mechanism I developed in response to dealing with the lack of control I experienced at the time. I remember being depressed and feeling lonely, having lost most of my friends from seventh grade. My recovery was painful, both physically and emotionally, and I felt misunderstood. My eating patterns drastically changed, and I found myself slowly fading into the shadow of Anorexia Nervosa (AN). *Anorexia Nervosa is a life-threatening mental illness characterized by behaviours that interfere with maintaining adequate weight. While the causes of anorexia nervosa are not completely understood, most medical and psychological professionals acknowledge that an array of biological, social, genetic, and psychological factors play a role in increasing the risk of its onset.*[1]

> *I felt so much more in control.*
> *Stronger than ever.*
> *Defiant to my mother.*
> *I was winning.*
> *Ninety pounds on the scale,*
> *yet I wasn't disappearing fast enough.*

At the age of 12, I wanted to end my life. I planned everything, including hanging myself in my wardrobe closet and the time I would execute my plan. When I was in the closet, trying to figure out the logistics of the scene, I received a phone call from my friend, Alexis. He was calling from his cottage. To this day, I recall this precise moment with so much clarity. I remember how I sat on my bed with my legs crossed, holding the landline phone to my left ear. I remember not wanting our conversation to end. He was so comforting, reminding me that I had a friend. I was so relieved, feeling the love from another. Alexis didn't know what was happening in my bedroom when he called. But thanks to him, I cancelled my plans to commit suicide that day. However, the craving for more meaning in my life and the feeling of never being fulfilled did not leave me. Fortunately, because I confided my desire to commit suicide in my sister, I landed at the doctor's office after a few days of reconsidering my attempt. I remember being so mad at her for telling my mother.

---

[1] Toronto General & Western Hospital Foundation, 03/21 nedic, National Eating Disorder Information Centre https://nedic.ca/eating-disorders-treatment/anorexia-nervosa

While sitting in front of the family doctor and beside my mother, I confidently lied about my level of food intake. I denied the pain I was experiencing. I blamed everything on my ski accident, the traumatic experience, the headaches and the stomachaches. I said I wasn't restricting; I said I was just not hungry. I pretended I didn't know what he was talking about when he suggested I was not eating with the hope of achieving the goal of losing weight. My mother and I silently left the doctor's office with a bottle of syrup prescription to ingest half an hour before each meal to increase my hunger. Needless to say, I was very meticulous at throwing the liquid in the sink for the first week or so. I became very diligent at not wanting to eat even more than I already had. Quite frankly, I did this in an effort to keep the control I had acquired with increased diligence, secrecy and strong will.

One tablespoon at a time, I kept my secluded behaviour alive. Despite my compelling desire to keep these dysfunctional actions as my allies, guilt and shame quickly came into play as I suddenly felt I was betraying my parents. I knew they wanted me to heal because they came with me to the doctor, and they wanted me to drink the syrup to get better. As a result, I slowly started to drink the syrup and began eating again in a way that seemed normal. I appeared to be healthy, but my eating disorder had another plan for me.

While attempting to heal my illness with my family's help, anorexia nervosa slowly evolved into binge-eating disorders behaviours. *Binge-eating disorder is characterized by recurring episodes of binge eating. It is important to note that overeating and binge-eating are not the same. Overeating can be described as consuming more food than your body needs at a given time. Most people overeat on occasion. Binge-eating is less common and is marked by psychological distress.*[2] My symptoms alternated between binging and restricting and then over-exercising. This transition was really hard. As much as I loved the high of restricting, I couldn't starve myself anymore, and it was painful. The inability to restrict made me feel weak; I wasn't succeeding at my own eating disorder, and I started to gain all the weight that I had lost. I felt like a failure because I still had my period every month, and I wanted them to stop. If they stopped for just a little while, that meant I was doing something right. When the menstrual cycle stops due to nutritional deficiency, it is a warning sign that the body is not functioning properly, and this should not be taken lightly. Still, I highly contemplated it as a reward. My bones were not visible anymore, and even if I wanted to, I could no longer make myself vomit after I ate.

I lived through many cycles of shame, guilt, self-hate, and self-sabotage intertwined with feelings of unworthiness, feeling *too fat and not good enough* for thirty-three years. I avoided dinners with friends, parties, drinks, social gatherings, dating, vacations, wearing a swimsuit in public, having my picture taken, and always comparing myself to others. Comparison to others was a way of invalidating myself, putting me on a lower scale of what beauty standards are supposed to be. In no possible way would I have dared to permit me to celebrate life. Just thinking about others, seeing what I thought was my undeserved happiness in them made me sink into complete humiliation. I thought they must be wondering how I could eat so freely, or not exercise, or how I could even exist and accept the body that I thought didn't meet society's expectations.

---

[2] Ibid

Obviously, I had signs there was something wrong with me; every flight I worked as a flight attendant I was asked if I was pregnant: *When are you due? Please, don't get that bag; it's not good for the baby!* After one of the last yoga classes I taught before going into treatment in 2019, a student excitedly exclaimed: *Congratulations, I didn't know you were pregnant!* Those comments followed me through my whole life—from the east coast to the west, from French to English.

> **Maybe I had to learn from them,**
> **but I had not found that lesson yet...**

Instead, I created a way to punish myself by using or restricting food to fill a void, hiding my pain and suffering. The cycle of my thoughts was unbearable, from wanting to restrict and binge eat, feeling disgusting and being culpable. I felt broken, ugly, old, and ultimately inadequate. To validate my inadequacy, I would pinch the skin under my arms, around my waist, my chin, and my thighs to remind myself *I wasn't perfect. I'm not perfect. I'm not perfect. I'm not perfect.* I sometimes *body checked* multiple times a day, and it was automatic if I went to the bathroom or anytime I faced a mirror. It was a compulsive behaviour reassuring me that I had not gained weight since eating last or a way to punish myself if I thought I had. Often, *body checking* was an attempt to remind me of the parts of my body I wished I could change or minimize because I would never focus on the parts that I liked. This was not because there weren't any, but rather because I didn't want to admit they were even part of me. Instead of providing relief, the body checking provided an array of emotions: increased dissatisfaction, greater feelings of loss of control over shape and weight, and an elevated level of anxiety and depression. I was obsessed with food: what to eat, what not to eat, when to eat, when to starve, what others thought of what I ate, and what others would think if I didn't. My body image expectations were high, yet I could never reach that ultimate destination. To be frank, I perceived any goals I set in the past as finalities; they were a constant moving target. This became very clear after reading Porta de Rossi's book, *Unbearable Lightness: A Story of Loss and Pain*. I finally related to someone who had the same illness—I never had before. Her words gave me the space to meet some of my shadows I have never wanted to bring light to because I have always been scared to explore them and find the truth that played within them. I read many studies on the subject of mental illnesses and also achieved a certificate in Understanding Eating Disorders from Douglas College in British Columbia. However, for as many studies and hypotheses surrounding the *why* and *how* of this mental illness, I never read anything about the subject that made me feel as understood and *normal* as her memoir did. It stirred up some issues I previously didn't want to admit about my identity and sexuality, but it helped me consider that it might be time to bring them to the table – or at least to start contemplating them.

Three summers ago, once again while lying in *Shavasana* during a yoga class, I wished I would fall asleep forever. I believed that if I could leave this plane, I would never feel the hate I had for myself anymore, and that the image I saw in the mirror would rest in the heavens forever.

And I cried. At 42-years-old, I was definitely aware of the reasons I wanted to fall asleep forever as opposed to when I was 12. My thinking mind was so different, my level of suffering was so different, and my knowledge of life was so different. The knowing of what would be missed was palpable. It was scary, way scarier. Yet, it was fine with me.

Somehow, just like three decades prior, when I wanted to renounce life and give in to the battle of depression and mental illness, I ended up at the doctor's office. The difference was that this time, it was without my mother by my side. I was by myself. *I'm exhausted*, I said. *I think I am depressed. I have anxiety attacks. And by the way, I don't know how to say this, but I have an eating disorder. I need help. I am dying from the inside.*

I felt so relieved to finally speak those words out loud, ready to make things better for myself, stepping into my healing journey. There was a huge desire to be free and share the beauty of life with my future beloved—to find a partner and not hide my authentic self anymore. I wanted to be comfortable in the uncomfortable and embrace life and help others embrace that same life together with me. I know the road trip to authenticity never really ends; it is a cul-de-sac, constantly circling toward the discovery of myself, and I wanted to fully experience that continual cycle. What if the resolution and answers to my inaccessible quest were lying there in front of me in my near future? Would I find what I have been seeking for so long? There was only one way to know—move forward. So many unanswered questions were popping into my mind.

Who is Julie when she is not self-sabotaging herself?
I didn't know.
Who is Julie when truly accepting and loving herself as she is?
I didn't know.
Would I heal through my treatment?
I didn't know.
Or would I relapse if I left the hospital without signs and symptoms?
I didn't know.

What I did know is that I wanted to move forward towards recovery. Even if all the experiences that shaped my past do not define me as a person, they definitely helped fabricate who I am today. I have clarified the person I am, how I want to feel, and what I need to do to be her.

Hungry to Surrender

Journal Entry
October 29, 2019

This is it!

I made it to the hospital. I was excited when my alarm came on this morning, and I realized where I was. I reminded myself that I've got this, and I welcomed positive affirmations coming abundantly through my mind one after the other: "I am going to get this thing done; I am courageous; I am going to nail this; I am going to succeed in this process."

Before I met with my friend Vanessa who accompanied me to the hospital for some support, I stopped at the bakery for breakfast and a coffee. I already had an idea of what my meal plan would be because I had a few phone meetings with the dietician. Her name is Hannah. She seems pretty young, at least younger than me, but she is really nice. I usually have no patience with nutritionists or dieticians, getting anxious and very "self-defency" with them as we don't have the same beliefs and knowledge—I admit that my knowledge is based on what I want to believe is right for me and not what is actually true and science-based. However, there is something about other people telling me what I should eat that I strongly dislike. I wanted to control myself when I went into the bakery and only choose one pastry. Still, after I ordered the muffin, a banana, and an Americano Misto with soy milk, I added a scone to the list, acting like it was for someone else—I didn't want to be judged by the barista. Sitting on a stool at the window, I faced Burrard Street so I could "people-watch" and be distracted by them, but mostly so no one could see me bite, chew, and swallow my food. I was mortified. Disgusted. Feelings of being humiliated by no one but me.

Sadness.
My eyes welled up.
The nervosity was kicking in.

I was so anxious that I ate everything without even tasting any bit of it. Except for the soy milk from the coffee drink, feeling its softness mixed with the taste of the coffee and hot water as it reached all four corners of my mouth, comforting me with a warm, familiar sensation. For a few minutes, I was torment-free while digesting my extra-hot beverage in silence until Vanessa arrived. I quickly remembered why she was meeting me here. We hugged a bit awkwardly, both being a bit lost for words in that context, and then walked towards what would be my new home for the next few weeks. Having her with me, I felt somewhat courageous but still tearful and emotional. However, when she left the ward and disappeared from my sight, I became lost and intimidated. Everything and everyone was foreign to me.

It felt so surreal. I felt like a five-year-old lost in a shopping mall filled with strangers during the Christmas holidays, looking for her mother. I experienced a huge cognitive overload. My lips *and face expressed sadness being on the verge of crying and trying to hold it together with my bottom lip quivering, just like when I was a child.*

Before lunch, I was quickly introduced to all the other patients while walking around the ward with a nurse who showed me around my new environment. My first meal wasn't a huge success. The eating area has a big table, so everyone eats together. When our trays are ready for us to verify, we check if the food on it is in line with our meal plan, and if so, we sit in our designated seat at the table—that will be my spot for the next seven weeks. My name is written with a sharpie on a piece of tape stuck on the table. This is a friendly reminder that I am in transition. It is a reminder that everything is impermanent, including me; I too, will leave, and someone else will take my place, the same way I am now taking someone's, and so on. The waiting list to get into this treatment program is more than six months. As I start my journey at this very moment, more than twenty-five people are waiting to sleep in one of the seven beds on the ward. From the moment my psychiatrist recommended me to my nurse practitioner after an evaluation, it took me six months to get here. I then received an assessment from the team here at St-Paul's and filled out various questionnaires before I was finally accepted. The sad part is that I am not the only one. The seven of us here at the ward are not rare exceptions; according to studies, approximately one million known Canadians suffer from eating disorders. This number is close to the population of Saskatchewan. Talk about a national problem. This is a real pandemic!

I rarely eat in front of other people without a load of anxiety invading my body. My chest tightens, and I feel like I'm under observation, needing to act or behave a certain way. I do not feel like myself and believe I should not be eating. There's huge culpability about it, and I have no idea where it comes from, but it has been with me for a long time up to and including this present day. I am acting, pretending to be all good about eating, but to this day, I still prefer to eat by myself. For some reason, it feels safer because I don't have to justify to myself what I am consuming and why, or even that I have to eat. Needless to say, I was upset and uncomfortable eating in front of the other patients, and especially at snack time, because I didn't want to eat the grains on my plate. I felt so guilty having those crackers with anxiety entering afterwards. I don't think it's healthy to eat cookies, and my habits do not include those kinds of things. At the same time, it felt good to eat something sweet, so I was a little bit trapped in my own thoughts.

They gave me magnesium intravenously, and I got nauseous and dizzy like I was going to faint. I had a really bad reaction, throwing up and doing everything in my power to hold the urge to have diarrhea. I haven't felt that degree of discomfort within all my being in a long time. I honestly thought I had a fatal reaction and that my body was shutting down. I am not scared of death per se, but I honestly thought I would die.. What went through my mind was how ironic it would have been if I died on my first day of treatment after finally getting there.

I think that eating six times a day is way too much, although I wonder how much more I actually eat when experiencing an episode of distress. I am trying to figure out if I will finally lose weight while here during symptom interruption. If I get to a place of coping in a healthy manner, I should be good. I made sure to tell them that if I gain weight here, we will have another problem to deal with.

I am exhausted, and I can't wait to just fall asleep tonight, but I have to wait for a snack at 8:30 p.m.

All the other people from the unit are so nice and welcoming.

It's 9:08 p.m. after evening snacks. I had a piece of toast with peanut butter and a decaf tea. It is so strange to eat before going to bed. I miss the taste of natural peanut butter though.

There is a girl here who was in treatment 20 years ago, and

she is back. I don't want to ask too many questions right now, but I wonder if she believes in recovery. How was she in between those years? I definitely want to ask her eventually.

Journal Entry
October 30, 2019

Man, I was sick all night. I threw up a few times. I wonder if it is the refeed process, the Magnesium, or the other supplements they gave me. Probably all of the above.

I couldn't go to the eating area this morning for breakfast, so I had my tray in my bedroom, but I couldn't eat anything. Everything was rolling around in my mouth, and I was nauseous. I thought I would have a free pass and not have to complete my breakfast because I was sick all night and still not feeling well, but that didn't happen. They do not allow any negotiation around being fed here or not; I had to drink some Boost to ensure that I received all my needed daily calories in my meal plan. I guess there is no way around it. It looks like I'm stuck and have to deal with my choices. I know I decided to be here.... but that doesn't make it easier.

I had to eat a veggie burger with a bun, and I cried. I'm craving vegetables, and I feel like I'm ballooning. I am not hungry during meals, and they feed me so many carbs— tomorrow will be either a macaroni dish or an egg sandwich. I just don't want either. I really want to heal, but I'm struggling. It is definitely an inner battle between my eating disorder and me, and as much as I am determined to get better, he is not a quitter either.

**I walk diligently with my horse in the dark forest,
illuminated only by the shine of stars in the clear sky.
Everything seems so quiet and peaceful at first glance**

in this magical woodland, but there is heavy noise in my mind.
I hear the howling of wolves far away in the background,
and the sound of their clamor agitates my mount.
They are warning me—they haven't quit the chase
as I escaped their ambush…
And they are gathering to discover a better way to find me.

Besides that, the nurse personnel is very nice and welcoming, but I am on the fence about the dietitian. Even though she is likable and very understanding, I have a hard time buying into all her theories and philosophy of nutrition. Within my irrational mind, I know more than she does. On top of that, I cannot be vegan here, so I have to switch my nutrition and be vegetarian. They don't allow cheese alternatives, but I can have dairy alternatives like soy milk.

I remember becoming a vegetarian and then adopting a vegan diet. At the beginning, the reason was for a different way of controlling my weight, rather than for ethical reasons. Even though the ethical reasons were high on the list, it wasn't my main focus. Instead, I was hoping it would be a magical way of eating, helping me lose weight, once and for all. I definitely related to veganism to help me be thinner, so my main motivation for losing weight would be fulfilled—any promise of weight loss had me restrict or eat anything that was required to do so. What is interesting to me, and I didn't know, is that research suggests people who suffer from eating disorders often become vegetarian; it is a way of easily restricting food while simultaneously being socially acceptable.

Research links vegetarianism and eating-related pathology,
such that prevalence of disordered eating behaviors
is significantly higher in individuals

who avoid animal products,
compared to omnivores. Vegetarianism may play a role
in maintaining eating disorders,
particularly anorexia nervosa.
However, there is insufficient evidence to determine if
vegetarianism is causal in the development
of eating pathology.[3]

As a child, I was a very good eater, and I loved food. I was healthy and always up for delicious food, especially at my grandparents' house and family social gatherings. My dad was an excellent cook; I can see him moving in the kitchen with the spatula in his right hand while dancing to a joyful song, whistling and moving from the stove to the kitchen table. As a family, we had such a great time on Sunday mornings, eating a whole loaf of bread, if not two, eggs, bacon, beans, cretons and sausages. There we were, the five of us, including my parents and two siblings, eating together, and I remember my dad being so happy to cook for us. He smiled, seeing us healthily and abundantly eating his food.

But I also remember me as a little girl, hiding to eat more food than was on my plate. I used to finish my brother's and, sometimes my sister's leftovers because I loved to eat, and it tasted so delicious. I never understood how they could simply stop when satiated. There were times when I ate under the table, not be seen because I thought I was overeating, and I didn't want anyone to know in case they might stop me from eating more. It's like I never had a limit when it comes to food intake—that feeling one has within the space between being hungry and full. I have always been curious how others

---

[3] https://www.sciencedirect.com/science/article/pii/B9780128039687000046

know when to stop eating. I was never aware of my hunger and satiation cues—when it was necessary to eat and when it wasn't. I was either super hungry or super full.

My parents separated when I was 14, just a bit after my accident. I always knew my parents were not meant to be together, and in fact, wondered what brought them together in the first place. I couldn't see how they fit as a couple, although, individually, they are two wonderful people. I have questioned whether this has affected my tumultuous love life; could it be that I chose relationships that never worked because I knew they would eventually fall apart as my parents did? I was never against my parents' decision to divorce because I saw that coming, and I now understand that they each needed to live for themselves and not just for their children.

Even though my father was an incredible role model, when I was 12 years old, I remember deciding that I would never marry a man. I took it even further, thinking that if I were ever to have a baby, it would be on my own and I would get inseminated just like the cows on my uncle's dairy farm. Ironically, I didn't even know that was actually a thing that human beings did, but I believed it was a possibility for me.

I knew my parents' relationship would not last, but I secretly wished they would somehow get back together. After they separated, I became hopeful when they tried to date again to see if they could make it work. They decided to go on a date, and my dad called the house before they met up. I answered the phone, and he told me he wanted to talk to my mother about the logistics of their evening at the Montreal Orchestra Symphony. I held the ancient black rotary phone a distance from my ear and felt the heaviness of it in my hand while telling my mother to pick up the phone. As I waited for her to come to the phone, standing on the second floor of the house just by the staircase, I quietly hoped they could work it out after all those years. It didn't happen.

During a recent therapy session, my psychologist asked me to express my anger. I didn't know what to do or say to verbalize it. I am not an angry person; it takes a lot for me to get to that point. It might be because I have mostly been a people pleaser, not wanting to offend or displease anyone; I think of myself as a relatively calm person. My way of expressing myself is by either sharing my love or emotions by crying if I feel upset or sad. If I am not displaying my best self-persona, I am mostly insecure and stressed, but I do not experience anger. The same thing happened when I was in therapy as a teenager. My therapist wanted me to scream to express anger, but I didn't have it in me. I didn't feel angry, so I didn't know how to do what she was asking or looking for. I blurted out some words that I thought expressed anger just for the sake of the experience and exercise. It felt inappropriate because I don't believe I've ever vocalized what I wanted or needed. She asked me to speak the same thing louder. And then, even louder. I was so embarrassed, but again, I didn't know how to tell her, so I just did what she told me. She asked me how it felt; I had no clue. But I figured out that me vocalizing an angry emotion was supposed to make me feel better. I didn't want to disappoint her, so I told her: *It felt good.* I lied to her, but I also lied to myself to please her and avoid telling her that I don't feel comfortable expressing anger. It's not that I can't be angry; it's just not a natural emotion I experience. I resonate with feelings of sadness, irritation, frustration, fear and hurt, but I do not associate at all with the emotion of rage. Another sentiment I cannot relate to at all is hate—I just don't understand it.

I often tried to pretend to be who I thought people wanted me to be; I did so unconsciously because back then, I didn't even know who I genuinely am. For a long time, I always presented myself in a good mood, pretending to be strong and positive, not bothered by uncomfortable situations around me, personal or not. When things became stressful, or I wasn't feeling good, I smiled harder—I learned how to *Fake it until you make it*. Besides my eating disorders, I also acted and used behaviours in ways that, to say the least, didn't serve me. I didn't know what I was doing, but I knew I was engaging in other types of addiction that made me feel good temporarily, like going out drinking and being promiscuous, giving me a false sense of being appreciated. I went to raves and danced all night long, which gave me another momentary false sense of the freedom I craved. I used drugs that would boost my serotonin and create brief euphoria, only to feel even more down a few days afterwards when fatigue, the lack of food, and the return to reality kicked in. I lived a lie while trying to make sense of a life filled with doing anything and everything misaligned with what made any sense at all! I don't regret any of these experiences because I wouldn't be who I am today if I had not lived them. I also would not be where I am today without the knowledge I gained, but oh dear, that was a long path of learning!

> *I tried to create a world around me with a certain tentative camouflage of protection, an embellishment of my reality that desperately tried to emerge with its true colours.*

So, when I arrived at the hospital, my behaviour wasn't much different. Yes, in the beginning, I was completely overwhelmed and back to feeling like a totally lost five-year-old. And this is something I have never really understood as unworthiness, self-doubt, and rejection manage to creep in every time, and I can't voice my needs or who I am. I feel like I'm that little five-year-old girl again. This reoccurred throughout my treatment, and I tried hard to figure out the association to that particular age, but it never came to the surface. Maybe I need to work on discovering what might have happened back then, so the significance can surface.

I moved through the period of adapting to the British Columbia provincial adult tertiary eating disorders program called North West[4] getting to meet everyone and feeling safer in my new environment. Along with this level of comfort, I started wanting to take care of the other patients by offering yoga classes, intuitive energy healing—Reiki—or Indian Head massages as I am a practitioner of these modalities. I asked the staff, and they obviously rejected the idea because it would interfere with my treatment; I was there to take care of myself, not consciously support the healing of others. Healing can happen through community, but this was not to be my direct mandate. I didn't realize it at first, but the hospital staff saw that I was creating a new mandate, to dissociate from my pain and disease by putting my attention on what others needed, just as I always did in the past. They recognized this pattern as they saw it in other patients doing exactly the same thing. I don't even know where I would have found the energy to take on such a project, so when it was refused, I was confined to more self-study and directed to start digging deep. I know this was why I was there, but my mind quickly wanted to default to old ways of functioning by rescuing others while in complete denial of my own demons.

During her stay in British Columbia, my sister participated

---

[4] https://mh.providencehealthcare.org/programs/
provincial-adult-tertiary-eating-disorders-program

in a meeting with my social worker and me to discuss the treatment phases I was going through. The logic behind this meeting was to develop good communication between my family and the staff to ensure that I felt supported during my hospital stay. We shared the next steps of my treatment, how things were going thus far, and my sister had the opportunity to ask any questions she had. My sister was the designated family member who was actively involved in my treatment; she communicated details to the rest of my family within this role. After meeting with the social worker, my sister told me a little bit about a telephone conversation she had with the social worker before coming to visit. Because the caregivers on the team had been working on this ward and in this area of healthcare for a long time, they could identify the kind of patient I was. They shared with my sister that they wondered when I might start to be more open and vulnerable instead of being effective and efficient within the program. I thought it was funny, although it hurt a little bit because I realized that I wasn't being authentic and real. I was, unconsciously, playing *the good patient*, but they saw right through me.

The point is that I wanted to succeed in my recovery. I honestly thought that I would complete my seven weeks at 4 North West, lose a few pounds along the way, and get healed. I had no concept of the reality of how ingrained the pattern of eating disorders was in me; I thought that if I just followed all the steps, hustled and bustled, and stayed busy, I would achieve success. I thought this was the formula, and there was no way around it.

So, my sister told me that the hospital staff was under the impression that I was playing the role of the *perfect patient*, being sociable and nice to everyone, smiling and being obedient by following my treatment plan and eating my food. In my head,

I was on a roll! I tried to be as perfect as I could be to reach the goals I set for myself while in treatment. Again, as I reflect on my journal entries, I shake my head, seeing how this was just a facade and how inauthentic I was. I put a mask on, trying to be a good girl, listening and abiding by the rules so I could please everyone. I wanted people to recognize my good behaviors and chose not to make waves instead of digging deeper.

However, I have to admit that since this particular program focused on a symptom and signs interruption treatment and I was barely using symptoms once there, I believed I was on my way to success. And that was my goal; I wanted to *succeed* in my recovery by following the outlined steps to achieve the goals and secure a title within the victory of achievement. Again, not sustainable.

I was also on a high because, after the second week, I was granted permission to go outside on the hospital grounds—success! Then, after the third week, I was given a pass, whereby I was allowed to go outside of the hospital property for an hour-long walk—double success! I used this time to go on fast-paced walks, knowing very well I was not supposed to exercise. With the goal to weigh less at the next weighing session, I was pleased that I started to feel hungry in between meals. My hope to lose weight contradicted the reason I admitted myself into this program, but I rationalized that being free of eating disorders signs, I could use overexercising symptoms during my passes to burn more calories. My intention to walk fast was used as a camouflage for exercise. I felt like I was winning, using the love of being active but not to enjoy a leisurely activity; losing weight was carefully intertwined within a different goal. I am happy to say that I am still a very active person to support my physical health, but I also enjoy the serenity of quiet, calm walks that nurture my emotional and mental well-being.

After a few weeks of playing with the system and using my passes to exercise, I told the staff after my Monday weigh-in that I was very sad my weight had not gone down, especially after all the walking I did. I felt I was losing control doing all this work for *nothing*. However, sharing this with the staff released the guilt I was carrying of not being honest with them, and it helped me get out of the shadow of my lies; it was time to be honest with myself. I think this is when I started to crack, bringing some light into my treatment by adding honest and meaningful work to it. At the time, I was not knowingly dishonest with myself because I didn't even know what I was doing. But there was something inside me at that point that told me I couldn't lie to those supporting me in the facility anymore. I had a deep knowing that it was time for me to be accountable for eating my meals and snacks and telling them about my whereabouts. I tapped into my genuine desire to get better, and I knew that I couldn't lie to anyone anymore because that would include lying to myself.

It always comes down to the dichotomy of choice—I discovered that at every moment, I always have a choice. I have always been curious about my resistance to healing from the eating disorder and why I would be so resistant to positive change. My therapists told me that it wasn't so foreign for people in treatment. For example, having dealt with eating disorders for 33 years, changing old habits into new behaviours takes some time for the brain to create new automatic patterns. I found an interesting article speaking to the push-pull of motivation and resistance that makes a lot of sense to me. Here is an excerpt:

Patients endorsing motivation to change. *When working with an adolescent or adult who is somewhat motivated to change her* *eating disorder behavior, individual therapy can be effective. However, recognition of the need to change behaviors and the ability and willingness to do the hard work to change them can be quite different. For example, patients with bulimia nervosa will often want to stop binge eating but are resistant to giving up the restrictive eating habits that lead to the binge eating episodes.*

One helpful strategy to deal with this type of resistance is to begin by working with the patient to identify what she wants to change and/or work on. This step may seem basic, but it can be overlooked by therapists and replaced with a presumption that a patient with an eating disorder agrees with the therapist's perspective and valuation. Achieving initial consensus on the goals of therapy and agreement to work on a particular problem/ behavior introduces a dialogue about how to achieve those goals. In treatments such as cognitive-behavioral therapy, the first session is spent building a model illustrating how the eating disorder is functioning for the patient. The model includes behavioral, emotional, and cognitive maintaining processes and illustrates the cyclical and dysfunctional nature of the eating disorder. The model is a working document and can be revisited during every session. As a result, it can be used to help the patient learn more about her eating disorder cycle, evaluate the effects of her behaviors, and address resistance as it emerges. As treatment progresses, the model can be refined and elaborated, highlighting emerging targets for treatment.

Conclusion: *Treatment resistance in eating disorders is complex and manifests differently depending on diagnosis, patient age, and duration of illness. These factors can inform the clinician about the types of resistance they are likely to encounter and on potential strategies and treatment options that may be useful in overcoming these barriers. However, the role and content of resistance will vary in each case; it is important to understand how each patient views* *her symptoms and the perceived function they offer in the context of her life. This understanding will help the clinician conceptualize why the patient is resisting and how this resistance is likely to interact with specific symptoms.*[5]

Cognitive behavioural therapy is usually the go-to treatment for eating disorders, and it worked well in my situation. As much as the illusion of relief of stress seemed to be alleviated by acting on the symptoms of my eating disorder, the illusion of control and relief was temporary, and I unconsciously knew that but didn't have the tools to make positive changes—I didn't know how to. Consequently, after each episode of acting on symptoms, I ended up feeling enslaved to the illness, enslaved to the part of me I knew I wasn't. It was the part of me that was unhappy and depressed and felt worse than before I acted on my urges. However, in 2019, I was highly motivated to change, and this is why I kept on pursuing my quest to live the life I always wanted, even though I wasn't quite sure what I wanted it to look like. What I was sure of, is that it wasn't the life I was living at that time.

---

[5] https://www.psychiatrictimes.com/view/patient-resistance-eating-disorders

Hungry to Transition

I was certainly highly motivated to change the life I was living in 2019. Even if I didn't see the light at the end of the tunnel yet, I was willing to do anything to find it. Everyday chores like doing groceries, cooking, cleaning the dishes, and house cleaning became more and more difficult; breathing and surviving were as well. It took extraordinary effort to ask my body, mind, and soul to find the little energy I had in me. All I wanted to do was to sleep. The only place I was feeling peaceful, free, and warm was in the yoga studio when I taught hot yoga classes. I would arrive early to experience the heat of the infrared light on my skin while listening to the most beautiful music, warming my entire being and forgetting who I was for a moment. When did I stop singing and dancing? When was the last time I became enchanted by a smile, a laugh, a story? Nothing phased me anymore.

So, going to the hospital was hard initially, but it was the most important thing I have ever done; that and going to Bali to backpack ranked as the two most beautiful gifts I have given myself. This was when I decided to take a break from life by temporarily slowing the fast pace I was living, along with everyday stressors like trying to pay my rent. I stepped back from being busy killing my soul, one destructive thought at the time.

A few days of proper nutrition and hydration triggered my body into some changes I didn't expect would occur from not eating for previous periods of time. One of the first things I noticed was the strengthening of my fingernails, and secondly, I produced more saliva while I ate! I never really paid attention to that before. It was like my body was saying: *Wait, what's this? Food? Let's just relish good mastication of whatever she is putting in her mouth!* My saliva glands never stopped functioning, and my salivary glands never inflamed, but I noticed a change in the amount of saliva that I was producing when I began eating more.

A lot of case reports describe non-inflammatory swelling of salivary glands
as symptoms of eating disorders like anorexia nervosa or bulimia nervosa.
They might be the only visible sign for the disease.[6]

There are a multitude of symptoms that can present in individuals managing eating disorders. They could include one or more of the following: fatigue, dizziness, low energy, weight loss or gain, abdominal discomfort, heartburn, heart palpitations, polyuria, which is expelling a large amount of urination in a day, polydipsia, which is the medical term for the feeling of extreme thirstiness, insomnia and amenorrhea, which is the absence of menstruation due to excessively low

---

[6] https://pubmed.ncbi.nlm.nih.gov/18253742/

body weight. Low body weight interrupts many hormonal functions in the body, potentially halting ovulation.

Most patients with eating disorders do not present with obvious signs during a physical examination. That was my case. Some people in my life told me they didn't realize I was not happy or that I was going through something so difficult. I often felt I was disappointing them by not meeting their expectations as I put a mask on to hide my suffering. Were they also disappointed that I was living a lie?

But at the same time, I was not fully living a lie, being honest through genuine happy moments shaped with them. Perhaps, I wanted to help them within their journey without sharing insight on my inner turmoil; I didn't have any outward eating disorder signs, but I still wanted to heal all my internal wounds.

For the treatment of binge-eating disorder and bulimia nervosa,
good evidence supports the use of interpersonal and cognitive behavior therapies, as well as antidepressants.
Limited evidence supports the use of guided self-help programs as a first step in a stepped-care approach to these disorders.
For patients with anorexia nervosa, the effectiveness of behavioral or pharmacologic treatments remains unclear.[7]

---

[7] https://www.aafp.org/afp/2008/0115/p187.html

Journal Entry
October 31, 2019

Last night, I slept like a baby. I woke up to go to the washroom around 11 p.m. and went back to sleep until 7:30 a.m. I needed four bottles of blood this morning. Apparently, my sugar levels are too low, and I may have to increase my food intake to regulate them; I pray they won't have to do that.

My electrolytes seem to be getting back to normal, but I have to continue the magnesium IV for the next four days. I feel bloated and a bit dizzy and nauseous. It's like I'm on a rocky boat and on the verge of throwing up all the time.

Yesterday, I began talking to my inner child again to help manage my struggles with eating at lunch—it actually helped me get through it. I held her in my arms while feeling full yet not done eating all that was on my tray.

I also started writing in my patient handbook, noting changes in my behaviour while enhancing my life, using the material I was provided.

It is very interesting to hear everyone's stories. All seven of us come from different walks of life, and we are so different from each other yet share that common "thing." We are a bundle of people who have the same deep issues of inner suffering. I feel no one understands us better than we can—because of our one commonality, we can relate to one another despite our differences.

I'm starting to get used to understanding my manual and selecting and planning my menus according to the guidelines. But I still think I'm eating too much, even though sometimes, like this morning, I don't think I have enough. I now remember that, since I was a kid, I was always afraid I wasn't getting enough food; my eyes were bigger than my stomach.

At this point, my desire to eat and my appetite are still very low. But I am required to finish what is on my plate, and I feel like a kid who is picky and fussy at the table. Sometimes, I wonder what the professionals really think of us. How do they see us? I am probably older than half the personnel here, and it is a very humbling experience to go through. They are professional women, and here I am, older than them, crying because I don't want to eat, desperately afraid to gain weight. It's even hard for me to look them in the eyes.

My body is so tired that I can't get enough sleep. But, on the positive side, I'm excited we are going to do some mindfulness walking this afternoon—I can't wait to go outside.

This evening, one of the patients—I will call her Lea—wanted to leave, and it was really sad to witness. She has been in and out of treatment most of her adult life, including last year. She has been here for a few weeks now, and she wants to leave halfway through her treatment because she doesn't want to keep going. She couldn't cope today, and it was heartbreaking to see her in so much pain and distress; the illness was taking over, and she wanted to harm herself. I just wanted to hold her tight in my arms. She is in her sixties—this illness does not discriminate. I never considered older people having eating disorders. I assumed I would be the oldest, at 44. But no, collectively, we are in our 20s, 30s, 40s, and 50s.

Since she is in her 60s and this is not her first treatment, I am in a lot of doubt about the treatment program and its effectiveness. I know we are not all the same with different backgrounds and sources of distress, etc. I wonder if it is like alcoholism or substance abuse, with some going back to consume, while others manage to abstain. However, I just realized today that only two of the seven people here are experiencing their first time in treatment—the youngest and me. I hope it will help her, and that she will be able to heal at such a young age and that she sees her own beauty and realizes that true happiness does not come from controlling food. I wish I had found the courage and the strength to go into treatment at her age. It is in times of hardship when I reflect on these things, and it makes me realize that not everyone has a similar journey, and my eating disorder may be curable; perhaps I will heal. I find it very interesting that I want her to realize all these beautiful things, but I don't follow my own advice or words of wisdom. Guilty.

Dee, a woman in my group who is approximately the same age as me, is so strong. At the very least, she convinced Lea to stay for the night and reevaluate in the morning, after solving this crisis. I see Dee as a true leader. She definitely would be the head of a group if we were in a women's prison. She is fierce, and I admire her strength and determination.

I also understand why some people still need continued support relationships after many years of AA meetings. I see it as help to diminish the odds of relapse and to increase the odds of survival. I see this happening within the community I am building, relating to what I am going through while sharing the hurdles I am experiencing.

Today, I feel quite a bit better, and I hope they don't send me home sooner as a result. There is a sense of safety being here with others with whom I don't feel threatened. And honestly, it is so nice to put my life on pause right now. I am finally starting to get a break from life as I start to unwind and settle into the ease of this process, even though I have strong fears about my body changing .

Journal Entry
November 1, 2019

I slept for eight hours with no sleeping pills, no melatonin, no Gravol.

When I woke up this morning, I was hungry. And I felt shame.

I was physically weak. What is happening?

Does my body actually want more food within this process of accepting it? I don't want to eat more. And then, when I got in front of my meal, I was not hungry anymore. I even had a hard time finishing everything on my tray: a coffee, an apple, one toast, one egg, honey and soy milk. And I still struggle with nausea.

10:50 a.m.—snack time. We're like cattle waiting for our meals and snacks.

I wonder why I'm still nauseous. I am less bloated this morning and have less water retention as well. My first few days were horrible. Apparently, that's what happens when rehydrating—adding water and electrolytes and simultaneously reintroducing carbohydrates into my meal plan. I learned it could be life-threatening to go through this dehydration cycle of dehydration and hydration while experiencing refeeding syndrome. There is a dangerous shift in fluids and electrolytes within the body, resulting in compromised cardiovascular status, respiratory failure, edema, seizures and possible death. It's eye-opening; I never really thought it could be that harmful. I mean, I knew that eating disorders ranked as the mental illness that killed the most, but I never stopped to think "how." Being healthy or avoiding being unhealthy wasn't my preoccupation.

Even though I know I've only been here a few days, I am conscious that eating still makes me nervous. I should be ok because my portions are controlled with no access to food in between our planned meals, and I'm not on a weight gain meal plan. But I can't help it, I'm a little bit uncomfortable about how my body will react to change and how things will stabilize; I wonder what my setpoint will be once I regularly feed myself. What if it is higher than I thought? Also, I'm not allowed to have a water bottle to fill at my convenience; I can use a water fountain with available small paper cups, but it doesn't seem enough for me. I feel I am not drinking enough water or eating enough veggies, and it drives me crazy!

I know they don't want me to gain weight, but I also know they do not want me on a diet to lose weight. I want to heal my condition of wanting to be skinnier, but I feel overweight, and that pisses me off. I know my BMI is higher than normal, which technically means I'm overweight; it hurts to know they won't let me lose that extra weight. I will be weighed Monday at 6:30 a.m., just like all the rest, and I would like to have lost weight. At this point, I am unaware of where I am at, having no idea how much I weigh now. I got rid of my scale because it made me paranoid. My preference is to check with the mirror and see how my clothes fit.

This morning I was asked to write a letter to my eating disorder like it's an actual person, which made me so emotional. I had to write to my eating disorder as if it was a "friend" first, and then as if it was my "foe." As soon as I finished the letter, I suddenly wanted to go into symptoms. But instead, I decided to come here and write in my journal.

Here is the letter I wrote to my eating disorder friend; near the end, I speak to it as my foe:

Dear eating disorder friend,

Although I feel I might have known you all my life, we officially met when I was 12 years old after my ski accident. However, I'm not one hundred percent sure when I first encountered you. You gave me power and strength in a time of my life when I felt hopeless and weak. I allowed myself to be silently assertive within my desire to rebel against the world. I proved to myself and everyone around me that, with determination and being inflexible, I could reach the goal I didn't know was in my mind; I wasn't even sure what I *wanted to achieve at that time. I was surprised how easy it was to initiate behaviours that I didn't know anything about; it just seemed that I knew what I was doing, and I had all the tools in the house to support me: a scale, a calorie-counting book tucked in with the aprons and tablecloths. I knew most of the rules, and what I didn't know, you taught me. Nothing else mattered except you and me. You helped me feed my urges to eat by motivating me to cook and make amazing snacks and deserts for my sister, so she could taste what I wanted without me absorbing the calories! There were bowls of ice cream topped with candy and chocolate cookie crumbles, and as I watched her eat with joy and delight, my life was falling into broken pieces like the bits of cookies lost in the melting ice cream. I wanted her to taste and savour what I defended myself to enjoy, not wanting to risk putting extra calories I didn't need in my body. You helped me intuitively count calories and know what not to eat, restricting when I didn't even know what I was doing. As a perfectionist and an excellent student, I was good at it, and I was so proud of myself. The euphoria of starving was embracing, and it cuddled me like heroin warms the blood of a junkie.*

I was making my father sad and getting attention from my mother. I thought she was jealous of my success. Having always been on a diet and exercise regimen, I thought she was jealous of my achievements, having found the secret to eternal youth and a perfect body. Meanwhile, she was struggling in her relationship with my dad and her self-image. You are strong and very powerful, and as much as I am attracted to your illusion of having power over my life, I realized over the years that this is a battle I could never win against you if I didn't take drastic and important measures to make my way into forced healing. As much as I admire your strength, I also hate you for making me hate myself and all aspects of my body; you made me feel unworthy of living a beautiful life. I thought you were serving me, but I realized that you were only serving yourself, wanting to gain power over me. I don't want to hate myself anymore. I am sick and exhausted, and I want to live a beautiful happy life. I want to stop pretending I am happy.

I see all the women here who keep coming back to treatment, and I do not want to be here five years from now. I want to accept myself, both physically and mentally. I want to live in joy and be more than five-tenths of my mood from now on. I want to burst into happiness in a non-judgmental way, live fully and love freely. I want to attract a partner who fully accepts me and wants to be with me without the condition of me losing weight. I want to live like no one is watching, and I want to be able to love myself and treat myself like I treat others, with respect, love and compassion. I always thought that "I" was the problem, but I now know that our friendship is the problem. This time, I am leaving you for good."

It is 3:00 p.m., and I had a meeting with my psychiatrist today, and she supported me in realizing that I am starting to take on the "strong Julie attitude" It is how I go to the "I am good" mentality to avoid going too deep. I get it. I totally started to wear that Superwoman's mask.. I actually felt really sad when I talked to my specialist. I told her how much I did not want to gain weight while I am here and how much it would destroy me. I asked her if I could be on a supervised healthy weight loss program. I had to ask her. She told me that they monitored weight, but there is no option to be on a weight loss program; that is not part of any of their therapy programs. However, it remains one of my goals and is one of the reasons I am here. My hope is that I get to the bottom of this. Of course, I need to heal my mental health first before thinking about modifying my body. I just thought they would both happen at the same time. I still have thoughts about what I perceive is the perfect body and that it will bring me happiness and the freedom to unlock the self-confidence I crave.

There have been so many times when I thought I would be happy or satisfied if only I lost ten more pounds, and I would reward myself when I fit back into those jeans. I convinced myself that I would finally be happy and confident in my abilities and capacities when I achieved a certain goal. I had the impression that if this or that, I would reach heightened happiness. Then I became curious about why I found it so difficult to live in the moment and be grateful for what I have. Why did I focus so much on what I don't have? Somewhere along my childhood and into my adult life, I seemed to have forgotten that my purpose in life was not to fit in a specific clothes' size, have a thigh gap, or reward myself only when achieving a certain version of success. I became this person who looked outside of myself for answers when I had everything I needed inside of me.

I had it. I had that knowledge, that wisdom within. I just had to figure out how to grasp its concept and bring it to the forefront of my life.

I have always been a very expressive and demonstrative person. My voice is strong, and my laugh is heard a mile away. If I were sad, I would just smile more. I wonder if I always acted authentically or how I thought people wanted me to act to not disappoint anyone. I was the one who had the positive insight to cheer people up. I have been told *I am too nice, too joyful, too loud, too present.* I was under the impression that I acted like a golden retriever, wanting to be seen, being friendly, wanting everyone to like me, and needing to be the *good* girl. But this is not who I am deep down inside me. I was moving lots of energy around and overdoing to please others and to be seen and accepted. And I felt I wasn't going to be seen or heard if I didn't create enough noise, when in fact, I'm genuinely a more quiet, discrete, and reserved person.

In 2019, after a few weeks of treatment, something seemed to shift. I felt more neutral, and I wasn't sure if it was a good thing because I didn't recognize myself as I began letting go of the need to react in a way that I thought was expected of me. For example, my sister came to visit me while I was at the hospital in early December, and at first, I didn't want her to come. I was concerned about the cost of the plane tickets just before the Christmas Holidays. What I didn't know, but found out when we reunited, is that my parents helped to cover the cost. I had the most wonderful visit with my sister! We did things we have never done together as adults, like going to restaurants and the movies. It was a beautiful visit.

On the day of her arrival, I went to pick her up at the Vancouver International Airport. I was looking forward to seeing her, and in the past, I would have rolled out the red carpet for her, jumping all around and running to meet her to show how excited I was. But this time, I was more subdued when I saw her coming through the sliding door. I made sure she recognized me from a distance, keeping my eyes locked on her silhouette as she walked towards me—I smiled even before she could see my lips. I walked towards her, and when I reached her, I hugged her in silence with all the love I had. An outsider would have probably thought this was a typical airport scene. Nonetheless, I felt disappointed that I couldn't demonstrate more excitement in her presence. I wanted her to feel validated for taking the time to come and spend the week with me. What appeared to be a lack of enthusiasm to me made me think that something was up with my medication: *Does it make me feel numb? Am I losing myself? Have I changed? Did she notice anything? Is she disappointed with my behaviour?*

The story I told myself was that she felt I was not grateful for the sacrifice and effort she made, travelling across the country to visit me.

The next morning, I expressed my concerns with my psychiatrist. Her answer was not what I expected, and even if she left me perplexed at the time—because I was certain it was about my medication—she was right. Being in treatment, I slowly came into myself without feeling the need to act in ways I thought people wanted me to. This supported me to be calmer and centred—more authentic. I didn't need to ask my sister if I had hurt her in any way because she didn't need me to roll out the red carpet to know that I appreciated her being there. She understood that because I was there to meet her and told her I was thrilled she was visiting, that was enough. I didn't have to be more, do more, or express more; just being me was enough.

I didn't understand or realize the shift within me, but it didn't take long before it sank in. I had an idea of how I wanted others to perceive me, and that perception of who I was supposed to be slowly faded away without me even noticing it. However, a few times during treatment, within moments of triggers, it did reappear. These were the moments when I thought I had to do more, be more, and express more for people to see me. I have to say that this behaviour is not part of my coping tools anymore. I have transitioned to a more reserved and calmer way of being. I humbly say that I can now express myself with my words and authentic self; my presence and genuine way of being are enough for people to see and hear me. It is a massive change in the way I show up in the world.

I have discovered that for any transition to occur,
something needs to shift within me.
I had to let go of the absolute desire of controlling
the situation I was in,
and I needed to start trusting the strength and
agility of my mount.
Despite our exhaustion, for the sake of our survival,
we could not let our persecutors win by default;
a proper and legitimate but peaceful duel was mandatory.

Everything starts and ends with my mind. I know that now, but it has been a long process for me to realize that I had the choice to be my own victim or my own hero. I talk about this in my chapter in the book *Daring to Share Chaos to Calm: Awakenings Through Covid.*[8] Having the ability to choose is not always that straightforward, even when the choices seem evident and simple. Sometimes, I need to take one move or step for others to follow—it's like a domino effect when I push that first domino, and the rest begin to move forward one by one. That effect can be both accomplished and interpreted, negatively and positively. For example, if I stop taking the path of recovery today and go back to using symptoms of eating disorders—because let's be frank, I am still pretty good at it! The domino effect will rapidly take momentum and can easily lead to a disastrous spiral. On the other hand, if I choose the path that serves me, that same domino effect will happen, but it will land in the victorious favour of my health.

Yoga greatly helped me in my process of healing. It supported me to take the time to be mindful of my senses and my thoughts. It allowed me to notice where I was at and

---

[8] https://www.daringtoshare.com/chaos-to-calm

acknowledge that, even if I wasn't where I wanted to be with a gap between my goal and the actual result, I could choose how to manage that gap, implementing the new coping tools I learned while discarding the old ones.

I can never repeat enough that recovery is not linear; this awareness supports anyone in recovery, those experiencing difficulties navigating it, and those not understanding what recovery is. Therapy and yoga helped me in what I could qualify as *experiential learning*. This is a process of education through *experiences* followed by reflection on those said experiences to use what was learned to adopt new behaviours.

I left the hospital to go home on December 17, 2019, with this perspective and intention in mind.

Hungry to Persevere

Journal Entry
November 6, 2019

There is a lesbian in our group. I talked to her about having some hesitation and questions about my sexual orientation and that I am not sure I'm one hundred percent heterosexual. I also mentioned it to one of the interns but asked the latter to keep it out of my file for now because I am afraid other nurses will judge or see me differently if they know I am attracted to women. I'm worried they will think I'm attracted to them, and I don't want to make anyone uncomfortable because that will make me uncomfortable. The same applies to the other patients. I guess I fear the possibility of rejection if I admit I am gay, just like I felt rejected by a friend when I was younger. After we kissed a few times, she told me she didn't want to do it again. She said she didn't want to be a lesbian. I was only ten years old, but I respected that. Of course, I was disappointed, and I felt cowardly. Needless to say, I didn't want to be a lesbian anymore either. As I removed myself from the lesbian world, I instantly felt like something was buried inside of me, something that should not be revealed or expressed. *I became a heterosexual by default, and to protect myself, I blocked any hint of my homosexuality.*

I've always been intrigued by the feminine connection shared between two women. Somehow, I felt they were lucky to fully express their love to each other by freely holding hands in the street and loving whoever they wanted. When I contemplated two women as a couple, I felt the softness of a gentle and tender feminine touch holding my hand too.

This is why I resonated with Portia de Rossi's book in every way. It hit home because I experienced the same emotions I interpreted from her writing. I understood that she experienced the same as I did, holding back in my life because of my sexuality. Her book exposes the dysphoria and isolation that accompanies a life lived in the closet and seems to be aggravated by her determination to be thinner.

Portia alternately starved herself and binged, all the while terrified that the truth of her sexuality would be exposed in the tabloids. She reveals the heartache and fear that accompany a life lived in the closet, a sense of isolation that was only magnified by her unrelenting desire to be ever thinner. With the storytelling skills of a great novelist and the eye for detail of a poet, Portia makes transparent as never before the behaviors and emotions of someone living with an eating disorder. From her lowest point, Portia began the painful climb back to a life of health and honesty, falling in love with and eventually marrying Ellen DeGeneres, and emerging as an outspoken and articulate advocate for gay rights and women's health issues. [9]

---

[9] https://www.goodreads.com/book/show/9219901-unbearable-lightness

For once, I felt I was normal. For the first time, I realized why I was like that. If I wasn't living according to my values, desires, and true self, how could I have deep relationships and live an authentic life? If the signals I was sending to the universe were not clear, how could I be aligned with what I truly desired? This book was a huge revelation to me and helped me start putting together more pieces of the puzzle needed to create the big picture.

This book was crucial in helping me understand the fight I had with me and my body. It helped me continue finding hope in the smallest space, and each time I did, it provided me with more and more self-awareness. One realization was that the outcome of my past relationships started to make sense. Most of them didn't seem authentic or have any real depth. I tried to believe they were genuine, but instead, I adapted to fit the persona I believed was expected of me. It felt like the relationship was happening on the surface, without any profound significance, and I watched from above and outside myself. All my past relationships were heterosexual and far from satisfying, void of a soul-level connection. I thought I was expecting too much, or I was too picky. I believe I was looking for relationships I knew would never last.

Of course, it was difficult to feel complete within any relationship, given I was never entirely comfortable in my skin. I rated myself based on the person I was in a relationship with. In particular, my mindset was that people would think higher of me because I was with a handsome man who had a beautiful body. It was incredibly superficial, but I was unconsciously seeking validation to fill a void within me. I essentially traded my authenticity for fitting into a mould I thought was made for me. I now realize that, since I was emotionally unavailable, I chose emotionally unavailable people. Over time, it became obvious I had to learn how to be emotionally available in order to attract the same in someone else. However, I was also in constant fear of experiencing meaningful connection, and I found myself in the space of chasing what didn't honour my higher self or expressing my values and what I really wanted in life.

I ended up expecting so much from others because I used them to fill my void, not realizing that I needed to put myself first and fulfill what was missing in my life. I now see how I jumped into these relationships only seeking what supported my emotional survival. That meant taking and giving only the part of me that didn't matter. I freely gave my physical self without being deeply connected and fully invested in the person I gave it to. At the time, I was unaware that I was chasing validation from them for my body first and foremost. Within the need to feed my ego to survive, I got lost in the lack of mutual respect with each man. I felt lost, even though I didn't know why, but I knew I had to change what I was chasing if I wanted how I felt to change.

Just like my relationships, I felt the trajectory of my horse
being misled by the sentiment of blind confusion.
It was as if I did it on purpose to shield his sight so he couldn't
see where he needed to lead me next—to hide
the direction of our true destination.
Unknowingly, I made him waste time,
directing him to stop at every roadblock,
pretending to be distracted so we couldn't reach
the end of our journey of self-discovery.
I literally preferred not reaching my journey's end
rather than discovering my truth.
He anticipated each hidden trap and detour like an ambush,

biting his ankle and making him bleed,
delaying any healing progress along the journey.
His sixth sense could smell the perfume of this ambuscade
amidst our combined disorientation.

For my own sake, I had to stop these soul-less encounters filled with instant gratification, pretending it was enough for me. What I was truly yearning for was a deep, meaningful, loving, and caring soul connection. I wanted an affectionate, loving, genuine, honest, authentic, and loyal partner. Unfortunately, none of what I was doing was making me happy. I knew these men only used me for their advantage, and I used them to distract myself from what I genuinely wanted. Letting go of my false sense of being and feeling desired wasn't easy, but I was slowly and surely stepping away from discomfort and heartache. I gradually began playing my own hero and stopped crying over fuckboys—this was undoubtedly one of the most empowering transitions in my life and journey. When I decided to protect myself and believe in me and what I deserved, things started to shift. Because I finally knew what I had to offer, I chose me and my power.

I desperately had to stop and fill my void, including all the expectations I had on others because, if they couldn't or wouldn't meet them, I blamed myself. I wanted what I thought was their love, their affection, their attention, their validation: That's what I thought I needed to feel worthy: the oppression, domination, obsession and the fierceness of the power of beauty I wanted to be. I will be honest, it was all about physical appearance, about being young and beautiful. It became a deemed survival instinct of sadness and obedience from which I craved to dissociate from.

As I write, I realize I have always valued the opinion of

others so much that it affected my behaviour towards them and how I viewed myself. I wanted to please; I am a people pleaser. However, even within their expectations of my promiscuous behaviour, there was a point where we established a mutual understanding that if I gave them my body, they would provide me with the sense that they desired me. This all came back to my measurement of the worthiness of my body. The smooth, sweet, oxytocin feeling of being physically desired equates to my body being valued as a currency of some kind. When filled with this fake dopamine, I would forget and survive the chaos for a brief moment.

Journal Entry
November 23, 2019

I got my discharge date: December 17, 2019, 10:30 a.m.

I went swimming today. Swimming in the pool of the unknown, I see two straight lines in front of me in the bottom of the pool, leading towards the depths of the waters ahead. Unfamiliar. Unnamed. Scary.

What if? Should I? Could I? Can I swim towards the foreign lands calling me? The ocean of my own eyes is reflected in the bottom of that body of water, representing the direction I can take. The choice encompasses my responsibility to either move forward in that lengthened direction or swim back to the shallow depths of fake safety, making me drown as if in quicksand.

I am here, holding my breath as I leap towards my own shadow while busting the myth of the unknown. Without apology, I feel the pearls of sweat coming out as my truth—coming out of my body and shining in the moonlight where I used to hide, and no one ever saw me. This is where my eyes shine like the sparkly stars of the

Milky Way, where my fingertips draw a constellation pointing in the direction of the firmament of my hopes and dreams.

My stay at the hospital allowed me to create space to get to know Julie a little bit more. It took time before I started to reach the part of me I didn't know very well. But once unfolded, I couldn't unsee, unfeel, or ignore what I was learning about myself. In a way, I was surprised at how my brain started processing the information I was being taught! It wasn't easy, but that may have to do with the situational motivation aspect and my readiness to experience the freedom of being healed.

Being hospitalized for seven weeks really helped me; I actually like it here. It gave me the break from life I needed—a pause from all the stressors living inside me. I had so much to do, providing little time to live life. Once I stopped playing the good patient and obsessing about things I didn't have control of, I was able to slow down a little bit.

Journal Entry
January 8, 2020

I honestly thought, desired, wanted, prayed I would be healed after my seven weeks in the hospital. But since I was not, I wanted to move on and pretend that "all was good," that I succeeded, and I didn't need to go to Vista Discovery. This is what I mean about not being authentic; sometimes I think I am, even when I'm not. Inside, I just want to go back to life and pretend everything is fine, when, in reality, it is not. I think it is the perception of having failed my healing, and yet, it's so fucked up because I genuinely want to succeed at my recovery, but at the same time, I don't want to fail at my ED. Oh, the dichotomy of it all!

I got a call from one of the psychologists in charge of the Discovery Vista program, letting me know there was a spot available for me at the end of January. I took the place of one of my Readiness co-patients because she decided not to go at the last minute. My head was spinning because it was way sooner than I expected. Three people were before me on the waiting list, but I got the invite almost three months earlier than I thought I would. I was even warned that it might take longer, so I was a bit taken by surprise and, initially, wanted to refuse so I would have more time in between treatments. I felt trapped and wasn't sure what to say. We can refuse treatment just one time due to circumstances with a work schedule. But I was and still am on disability, so I could not use that as a reason. I had one month to prepare, having to start at the end of January.

Readiness is a very well-organized six-week program in between the treatment at the hospital and Vista House. Before I started, I tried to visit every week, sleeping at the house the night before, so I was already there in the morning. I got to meet the staff and the patients, known as the residents, so when it was time for my actual treatment, I had met almost everyone. This made it less traumatic, eating with others and going to pre and post-meal groups and other activities. It was really intimidating to watch those who started there before me because I know how the eating disorder in us likes to compare ourselves to others: our size, beauty, and progress in recovery. So, I wondered if they were measuring their progress with new recruits in the program or if they were past that? In the end, I managed to say: "Yes" and took the January 26th spot. There was no going back.

Well, I did have the choice to go back, but I'm proud I chose to be my own hero instead. And now I'm excited. Stoked. There is peace within a little bit of hope again, which is what I need to sustain me until the next time. With this comes just enough resilience to support me in creating a game plan.

So, I am looking forward to spending another 12 to15 weeks of treatment, but this time at Vista House. It will be a little different this time because I will have my own bedroom, and that is certainly a plus! I feel good that I met everyone in the house ahead of time, yet, I still have some uncertainty about how I will fit in and if I'll be accepted as I am. But I am certain it will come in time. For now, I am going home to spend a little time getting ready for my new adventure. I will follow the meal plan I currently have and continue the hard work.

I remember my discharge day like it was yesterday. I was relieved, yet I didn't want to leave the comfortable nest I evolved in for seven weeks. With the help of the staff at 4 North West, I was able to rest, learn, and stop most of the signs and symptoms of my eating disorder, creating a better day-to-day life. I was under the impression that this little haven was the tiny bubble of protection I needed to survive. I wondered:

What if the wolves were outside the sliding hospital doors,
waiting to find me again?
I have a perfectly clear image of them.
Each is covered in beautiful grey fur with one clean,
brilliant white patch on their stomach.
I imagine the red, almost purple blood of their victims
tarnishing the purity of their coats.
Their claws are ready to grip their prey,
and they bear their long,
pointed fangs designed to easily puncture their kill.
They have magnificent eyes with the keenest vision
meant for vast distances.
I hear them howling, and they become more and more
territorial and tenacious as they wait for me to come out.

Journal Entry
December 17, 2019

Today is my discharge date from the hospital.
Weight: 157 pounds.

I am the same weight I have struggled with my entire adult life, the number I have fought all along. I don't understand. I made so many efforts. I worked so hard. All that for nothing, just to go back to square one?! I felt so good about myself when I left the building and before I saw that number. I felt good, not only physically but mentally and emotionally as well. I thought I lost weight, and I was going to keep it off and continue adopting good habits without being self-destructive.

I'm baffled. Was it really all in my head, the idea that numbers had to guide and dominate my life? I feel many different emotions: accomplishment, sadness, love, hope and fear...and more fear. And hope. Fear. Hope. Fear. Hope.

It was emotional to say goodbye to everyone while dragging my overloaded suitcase, waiting at the elevator after my last morning snack at 10:15 a.m. It was raining when I departed the hospital. I have a cold. My lungs are congested, and my throat is dry. I have been coughing a lot. I am never sick. Go figure. It's probably the stress of the past week, knowing I was leaving with every day a countdown, always wondering if I was emotionally and mentally ready to leave the comfort of the 4 North West. But I was definitely looking forward to sleeping in my own bed with no roommates.

I planned a night stay at the Vista Discovery House facility, where I met with the other patients. I had dinner, then a post-dinner group, breakfast in the morning and my last "readiness" group before being qualified for admittance to the house. Lastly, I had an appointment with the nutritionist to see how my food log and meal plan were going.

It is hard to put a word to how I feel. On my way to the Vista House, it was raining, and I could not use an umbrella because both my arms were full with my suitcase and carry-on. I was supposed to eat before I got there but couldn't find a "safe" place to stop, feeling too febrile and fragile to find somewhere that inspired me, so I went directly to the house. Unfortunately, I took the wrong way, so I had to walk longer, and I was sweating, being overdressed and hungry. There were a few restaurants along the way, but I was too overwhelmed to stop for takeout.

I arrived at the house at 12:45 p.m. instead of 2 p.m. All the patients were already at St Paul's Hospital for the day, but I wasn't too overwhelmed meeting everyone because I knew most of the patients. Suzanne was the nurse who greeted me. Her smile warmed my heart, and her understanding and compassion provided a beautiful vibe. She made me feel at ease. She made me feel so welcomed, and I will never forget that moment. She asked me if I preferred to have lunch at the house instead of going out in the rain, and I was so happy she asked because I would have gone for a walk without eating if she had not asked me to stay and eat with her. She helped me make a sandwich, and then I went for a three-hour nap before we started the pre-dinner group. I didn't want to wake up from my slumber.

I was so nervous, meeting the other patients for the first time. Even though everything went fine, I felt like a five-year old, wanting to belong so badly; I feared being rejected, but everyone made me feel so welcomed. I didn't sleep well because of my coughing, but I am happy to have some privacy compared to the more public environment of the hospital. I look forward to coming back and living here for 12 to 15 weeks. The other patients were surprised I came right from finishing 4NW, reinforcing that I am committed to my recovery plan. It made me believe that I've got this and I'm on the right path to start "Readiness!" In my heart, I know I NEED that support, and I want to get as much as possible before the Christmas Holidays because there won't be any group for two full weeks before "Readiness" resumes.

When I saw my weight on that discharge sheet, I knew why the hospital staff didn't want to share it with me during my hospital stay. Their discretion was mandatory and necessary for my recovery process so I could focus on my well-being and nutrition and stop the signs and symptoms during my hospitalization. You never win with an eating disorder. I didn't want to acknowledge it, but the psychiatrist nurses know. I went to treatment to try something I haven't in the past and take a new approach in healing to get a different outcome from what I had in the past.

I do not want to live my life using a number to dictate every step along the way. I do not want to live the rest of my new life, hanging on a cliff, not knowing if I will be pushed away by the strong wind of the eating disorder or be saved, if only for a few days, weeks, months, or years.

In a way, my sneaky eating disorders helped me to heal—if I went to rehabilitation, I could stop binging and lose weight, or so I thought. I didn't lose weight per say; however, it made my body start to trust me for a long haul, and we were just at the beginning. My body now hopes I will continue feeding it, and it seems to appreciate the food I give it to help keep it alive.

Maybe this is life's way, or even my body's way, of telling me I need to be resilient and trust that this is the way I want to live. I need to be comfortable, thrive and be healthy with the energy required to manage day-to-day tasks. I am trying to be strong despite still coping with an internal fight. The positive side is that I can't unlearn what I experienced and accomplished during my stay at 4 North West, realizing what I really want my life to look like *without the struggles, the constant fight, and self-hate. I will never forget why I went to treatment in the first place, and I will keep an eye on the prize, a.k.a—freedom.*

I took the ferry back home, and as I held my coffee tightly during the ride, I thought about my new adventure. Once again, coming back home from my stay at the hospital was a double-edged sword, providing an anchor of learning, along with the challenge of implementing those lessons in the real world.

> **Life is filled with such dichotomies,**
> **but I discovered that every victory comes with**
> **a few doubts and a U-turn or two.**
> **I also learned that every epiphany**
> **takes me one step closer to a victory.**

Journal Entry
December 20, 2021

I don't know what happened to the hope I had once I got back home from that trip, but I quickly returned to my ancient ways of managing stress. Those coping mechanisms came back in full force, and I didn't know what to do. I didn't change my medication, and yet, I wanted to upload more pills down my throat. I was obsessed with my body image and had to get rid of my mirror, which was a blessing in disguise because it didn't serve me in any positive way. I started by turning it around and creating a dream board on it. So, for the next while, I taped all my goals on the back of the mirror, and it served a purpose. However, one day, I had enough, and I placed it in the local ads. It sold rapidly, along with my weigh scale. I didn't even check my weight or have a last look in the mirror before I sold them. Another victory! I don't think I should have a scale in my house anyways because it plays with my head, and I am facing a bit of a U-turn. I haven't had an episode of overeating in more than eight weeks when I slipped the first day I returned home from Vista during a period of isolation.

And then, I had an episode with some muffins I made. Since I was a child, I loved the muffins my mother baked. They are nothing special made with Kellogg's All-Bran and some added dates or raisins sometimes. Not very surprising, they are a very comforting food for me. So, for a moment when I felt lost and isolated, I went with what I know best and used emotional eating to cope. The muffins distracted me from my genuine desire to connect deeply with someone to express how I feel. And that is ok. Providing myself with the space of acceptance and self-compassion was a new tool I learned during my stay at the hospital. I never felt more human than when I took this turn in between 4NW and Discovery Vista because I learned new behaviours and ways to cope after a binge and/or an episode, and I was able to be vulnerable.

I read that pursuing an addictive behaviour is part of the brain being hijacked by a substance or a behaviour. *New research suggests that the brain's reward system has different mechanisms for cravings and pleasure. Craving is driven by the neurotransmitter dopamine. Pleasure is stimulated by other neurotransmitters in "hedonic hot spots." When we crave circuity overwhelms the pleasure hot spots, addiction occurs, leading people to pursue a behavior or drug despite the consequences.[10] In a sense, addiction is a pathological form of learning,* says Antonello Bonci, a neurologist at the National Institute on Drug Abuse.[11]

---

[10] Smith, Fran. The addicted Brain, National Geographics, September 2017, p.42
[11] IBID

I experienced a shift in perspective and how good it felt when I started being successful in my recovery, even if it was not linear. I try to remember that I have the choice and changing habits is the key to success. I always have an option given what I know at a specific moment in life, and until I learn otherwise, I will act depending on how I know how to cope—this is emotional survival.

The help I got from professionals changed my life. I wanted to succeed, and, as strange as it seems, I wanted the professionals who supported me to be proud of me. I built relationships with them, and it still feels difficult to admit that I sought approval from them through their recognition of my successes. *You are doing so well*, and *I am proud of you* went a long way with me. At the beginning, I thought they were praising me because it was their job—and honestly, I know it is. But, by counting on my caregivers' validation when they commented on my rapid progress, I minimized my success by not accepting accountability for my accomplishments.

A force of positive change happened when I chose to go to the transition home. In the past, I consciously wanted things to change, but my limited beliefs filtered the information I wanted. My subconscious would not allow change because of what I believed about myself—lack of self-esteem and poor body image, to name a few. I always thought that if I were thinner, I would feel more beautiful and have more self-confidence. This would, in turn, create the happiness and success I wanted. During my healing process, I was resistant to share my success with other patients; I was apprehensive, thinking they would view me as arrogant if I talked about my victories. I had a hard time admitting that I was striving to be a courageous hero rather than a victim. In my mind, I constantly question where the false belief came from that a woman can't be mentally, physically, and emotionally healthy. Why can't she be victorious, prosperous, authentic and brilliant? Why do I think I need to be thinner to achieve happiness and be loved?

I have learned that thriving for progress served me better than thriving for the abyss of perfection.
I also know that as long as I am not aligned with who I truly am, I will suffer from not remembering who I was born to be.
I want to live a fulfilled and beautiful life where I play a massive role in creating freedom for myself and others.

It was time for me to step entirely outside of victimhood. I needed to de-program what no longer served me and rewire my brain so I could be the best version of myself and take my power back. It was time to transition and say Yes to life one more time because, as Courtney C. Stevens says, *Nothing changes if nothing changes.* So, with this mindset, I started my second treatment on January 26th, 2020.

Hungry to Trust

Behind the armour I wear—this sturdy silver bulletproof carapace—two strong forces reside in me and fight each other. They are divided into two fierce desires: to live and to die. I question whether or not I should remove this shell that has protected me from being my authentic self for 33 years. It has allowed me to hide my identity because I never wanted anyone to see my skin, my body, and my dying soul. Pleasure, joy, and love were foreign to me and too scary to accept or hope for, while deception, abandonment and rejection were too high a price even to consider. I knew the cost of each side. I knew both choices had consequences, and neither was an easy decision to pick and stick to. Neither would be easy, but again, I was ready to look underneath the sturdy silver bulletproof carapace and face the limited beliefs that covered the behaviours I always adopted: starving myself yet, always wanting to be sure there would be enough; not enjoying food and eating fast; losing control without letting any joy creep in; numbing any feelings; and the obvious one of not allowing anyone to see any part of it. I felt despair as I managed my distorted body image with accompanying shame; it made me feel like a pig—double the shame. And then appears the guilt of ruining my diet... tomorrow, I tell myself. Tomorrow is the magic word when I am in destructive behaviour mode: I will start again and do better tomorrow; I will go on a fast or a cleanse; I will do more yoga and go to the gym. This is the cycle of my life. The destructive thoughts come back at me like swords in my chest.

Reason dictates that I should not be overwhelmed with the dichotomy of choices between recovery or illness when these two scenarios present themselves. I wouldn't hesitate to choose freedom, healing, and love had my mind not been programmed to years of coping mechanisms more destructive than favourable to my overall wellbeing. I wouldn't even be here writing about it. But, I have been living on a rocky boat for the past 33 years. It was certainly filled with sunny days, but there was also some stormy, overcast weather, during which I pretended the sun was shining. I became exhausted in ways I didn't think possible, living what I thought was my reality for so long. When I realized this, I knew I wanted my life to change; I wanted my story to change. This is why I decided to go to the inpatient recovery center facility with seven other patients on January 26, 2020, one month after being hospitalized for seven weeks. The program at Discovery Vista House[12] was divided into two parts. I spent weekdays at the hospital, working one-on-one and in groups with professionals and evenings and weekends, living with a community of other patients, learning how to meal prep, cook, and cope with eating at the table with others. I learned how to create a more diverse meal plan and received support around eating *fear foods*.

I thought 2020 would be my year because of the positive

---

[12] https://keltyeatingdisorders.ca/vista-eating-disorders-treatment-program/

changes I planned to make in my life. I know life rarely unfolds the way one predicts, but 2020 was a different year for many reasons, and its challenges affected my time at Discovery Vista.

Journal Entry
January 31, 2020

This is the end of my first week at Discovery Vista. I was one of three patients starting at the same time last Sunday. I feel reassured and safer in a way because we were all in Readiness together and now new to this facility. Having a little bit of familiarity was very comforting in this unexplored territory.

We all have a cooking partner, and like most of the other patients, mine has been really welcoming to me. Each of us has an evening when we cook between Monday and Thursday, and mine is on Thursdays.

Even if I see all the good in the different challenges and hurdles I experience, my first week was quite hard. On my first cooking night, I had to make macaroni and cheese, which consists of two of my most feared foods: pasta and cheese. Preparing the meal wasn't that bad because my cooking partner made it easy for me by cooking it. This helped me, but when it came to presenting the dish to the other patients who were not really excited about it for the same reasons I wasn't, I felt rejected and took it personally. As a result, I created a story in my head that they weren't open to my cooking, thinking they didn't want to eat my food—I was so distraught. I tried to hide my tears when I got in line to get served, but I had to go to the bathroom for a few minutes to ground myself. When I came back to the line I was still unable to contain my tears. I cried at the table with what appeared to be a gigantic mountain of pasta topped with milk and cheese on my plate. I couldn't swallow my food because I was trying so hard to hold back my tears. I knew I had to finish my plate—that's part of the rules. I tried to hide my pain, which made it harder to contain the suffering inside my core. I was doing something against my will, and it felt like I had no control over my life. I felt like that shameful five-year-old again. The shame: Who does a meltdown at 45 years old about not wanting to eat pasta and cheese? It made me feel like I was a little kid not being understood and seen and that I had to swallow and suck it up. However, the staff was amazing, and I felt supported and held.

I can just feel it in my core again, eating while my body is rejecting it, and the tears drop from my cheeks to the pool of cheese on my plate. My rational mind knows nothing will happen, but my unconscious mind and the eating disorders really believe a catastrophe is about to happen in my world.

We have 45 minutes to eat our dinner. Then, every evening, we have post-dinner group meetings to describe our day. This activity is a distraction and supports us to focus on something other than what we just ingested. It also creates a sense of community, so we do not feel alone or tempted to use symptoms like vomiting after eating.

Examples of the questions asked during our post-meal group include: How was your day? What are your victories? I always feel like I am bragging when I share my victories out loud in front of others. However, my conscious brain can see that it really helps the brain rewire: Good things are also happening during treatment, and it is important to see that part of the recovery so we can see the bright light and relearn that we have power over this devious illness.

More questions: What are the coping tools you have used? What are you grateful for? What are your plans for your evening?

The events that shook the world in early 2020 reshaped not only mine but every individual's life story worldwide—the entire population was affected. This was one of the reasons I was compelled to participate in an experiment to write about my experience during that time. It would be a legacy to myself, documenting my new vision of life as I witnessed and reflected on my growth in years to come.

I found myself drawn to discovering more about myself during the Covid-19 outbreak and how I could sustain my authentic self while navigating an ocean of chaos while being in treatment. I questioned whether I would drown in the deep waves of this illness during a pandemic or if I had the strength to hold on tightly to the raft that life was throwing at me. I asked myself: *Would I be able to live, survive and thrive, and find the freedom I craved if I could choose?*

Could I discover the art of coming back to life
while a pandemic surged around me,
or would I forever sink in the dark waters of non-liberation?

I feel myself constantly wanting to break free from that awful place of living within the fear of inauthenticity and unworthiness. When I am there, I hide or minimize myself, and that is the purest form of chaos. I want to break free from that space that thrives where the truth is meant to reside but gets hidden behind lies and surrounded by shame. I need to survive this race to be able to tell the tale that one can believe in miracles because fear is an illusion built in the fort of disempowerment. I want to be open to the mysterious unfolding of my life and uncover who I am—someone who is unpretentious and completely valid, even during a pandemic.

This pandemic has not yet come to a resolution, and before it does, I want to share what freedom feels like on my skin and how I think about it in my mind. Its flavours tease my taste buds as they dilute on my tongue without shame or guilt, and I breathe my freedom with conscious awareness, knowing I am not the prisoner of my thoughts or others.' This freedom includes acknowledging that I am not my illness, and I can choose the rhythm of my own galop, my own dance, my own speed, my own path—in essence, my own life.

I want to be able to share and express myself in such a way that, when others enter my world, they feel connected to it, and they can freely breathe and feel they belong in it. It's important to me that those entering my life get to know me, perhaps even more than I ever knew myself. This is about bringing the palpable freedom that is the blueprint of who I am and who was once hidden back to the surface and back to life so that I and others better understand me. There have been periods of time when I didn't know what to do with the feeling of being held tight up against a wall; when I lived silently against my values in fear of making too much noise and only listened to the predators in my thoughts who waited to eat me alive. I have a deep knowing that individuals will relate to my suffering, disturbing thoughts, feelings of guilt, shame, anxiety, and the resulting stress I endured. I can only hope that the words I write here in this book present a humble and vulnerable invitation for others to step into my world of thoughts, desires, and hopes. They all existed before Covid hit, and they are still with me as I continue to journey through self-discovery.

I felt that this chaos around me caused by the epidemic was and still is an illusion. My mind cannot grasp the context of it all, and my eyes don't see it as it appears to others. My soul sees it as another way for the entire world to be shaken and moved from its current state, a fight between good and evil, light and dark, the higher power and the fallen angel. It feels like a violent yet important message from the archives of my soul, telling me

I need to set free from what is not serving me so that I can return to my essence of being—back to my truth. Watching the world around me, I am in disbelief, wondering why nobody sees the same thing I do. I feel like I'm living in another realm, a parallel universe where only the complicated and misunderstood quantum physics laws apply. All parts of me believe the naked eye does not yet see an underlying and unexplainable reality. I can't explain it; I just know it. I can feel it. And I can see it...

I see it beyond my eyes—it's far, far away.
I am here, but I'm also there.
I am riding fast, feeling the movement of
the white horse underneath my seat.
My horse is moving at a pace that is faster than our heartbeats,
faster than the predators who want to
eat our flesh and drink our blood.
I feel like we are flying,
running so quickly on a two-beat stride with all four legs of this
determined animal off the ground at once.
I hold my swords towards the skies and scream for justice,
feeling the tears run down my face.
They draw the most beautiful canvas on my cheeks
before they land on the ground.
They are paintings of justice,
connection, assertiveness, worthiness,
peace, grace, purpose, but most of all,
they represent freedom.
I want to break free from the pain caused by the fear of
rejection, indolence, and self-hatred.
Breaking free will allow me to let go of
my ambivalences and doubts,
and my addictive and destructive behaviours.

I am breathless.

When I arrived at the transition house, Covid-19 was a foreign and far-away concept in my mind because I was more focused on working on myself than watching the news. I vaguely heard about what was going on from a few patients who began worrying about the virus taking over the world; apparently, it was more serious than the regular flu. People were dying, and some countries closed their borders. On Sunday, March 9, 2020, the pandemic rapidly became my reality when I was advised there would be no program the next day. Our care team was coming to the residence to discuss the program's future amidst this situation.

That next day, I was sent home, being told it was a temporary measure and I would probably come back in a couple of weeks to resume the program where I left off. I had completed half my stay at that point. I was certainly disappointed, but I thought it would be a great opportunity to go home and practice the tools I learned thus far. I thought I would make a conscious and mindful effort to discover what worked for me, what didn't, and what I still needed to work on. I was told I had to quarantine for 14 days, and the medical and professional team would re-evaluate the situation afterwards, depending on the Health Authority's advice. However, once I got home and the weeks passed by, I realized that I, like the rest of the world's population, was not going anywhere anytime soon but rather staying home.

I felt a lot of stress and anxiety over the social media hype about body shape and weight during the first swells of the pandemic. *Lose weight during a pandemic! COVID Diet. Pandemic Weight-loss Plan. Be in the best shape of your life. COVID-15.* I felt pressured to perform as people laughed about becoming fat or an alcoholic during the pandemic, while others made jokes about the producers of Biggest Loser or My 600-Pound Life contacting them after the chaos of Covid. I also wanted to start losing weight again because I didn't know how to deal with being alone at home. I felt unprepared and lost confidence that my 15-week recovery program was the key to getting my life back. Staying home with only online support was like going back to the dark waters of my pre-hospitalization. Feeling defeated and powerless, I was sure life was presenting concrete evidence that recovery was not possible for me, and I wanted to quit the program. I decided that I might as well go back to what I know best—restrict, binge, over-exercise, repeat.

What a waste of time. I needed in-patient treatment, but I was home. For the first time in my life, I felt injustice, anger and betrayal. I even felt incredibly naive and weak to think recovery could have worked for me. The eating disorder was striking back. It knows me so well, always following me, wanting to kill me and eat me alive. Food and my body are my worst enemies, and I found myself alone trying to recover with my two opponents. But I kept them at arm's length and fought with the little strength I had left.

I made a deal with myself; even though virtual appointments were not ideal, I concluded there was no other option as the program could not operate normally because of the pandemic. However, I was angry because, for the first time in my life, I felt I deserved to heal from that beast running towards me. I was in survival mode and being at home alone was not the type of care I was prescribed and truly needed. The relationships and the closeness I had with my peers at the recovery house began to dissipate. I felt our connection water down just like the program. I wanted to believe everyone was as committed as I was to the race against eating disorders, but I was wrong. It was a great hardship dealing with feelings of betrayal and grief, but I had to tighten the saddle and accept that everyone is on their own journey; even if we are in the same race, we are not in the same lane, and our battles are all different.

With each meeting, I could feel each person's competitive edge disperse—the eating disorder is evil. I tried my best at home, following the program, despite the lack of connection with others. I was very aware of my lack of self-care as I showered less and had zoom meetings with my naked chest secretly hanging loose in my oversized shirt. I set the camera in a position where no one could see how I was letting myself go. I counted the days back to when I last showered. I stunk. My hair was greasy. It felt like a competition with those on the calls to see who was struggling the most. The eating disorders were fighting hard to win: *Who is more sick? Who can't cope? Who is using symptoms? Who is following the guidelines? Who doesn't respect them? Why?* I felt naive and foolish to be so recovery focused. I felt resentful, betrayed, lonely, and weak because, ironically, I was one of the few following my meal plan.

One of my triggers is not having a set routine, and something I struggle greatly with is taking my medication in the morning. I was hesitant about starting medication, but if I don't take my meds, I want to disappear, so I never have to see my reflection in the mirror again. If I happen to walk by a mirror, I fat-check, wrinkle-check, and hair-check. On the worst days, I stay in bed, don't shower, and don't eat. I deprive myself in order to feel proud and strong. Then, suddenly it hits me, and I eat too much. Then I hate myself. One cannot survive without food, but it's a dilemma because I see food as my body's enemy—having either too much or not enough will kill me. And that is the problem: *How can I have a sane relationship with food?*

What supported me to experience success at the in-patient treatment house was that I wasn't burdened by extra daily chores, like shopping for food or preparing meals on a daily basis. I ate meals in a supportive environment and had post-dinner reunions with the other patients and staff to chat about our day. This was a great distraction as each of us unfolded the coping tools we used that day and shared our victories: what we were grateful for and our intentions for the night. There was always a staff member available 24/7 in case we couldn't sleep or felt distressed. I felt the support I waited for my entire life was taken away from me when I went into quarantine. And it was.

I felt selfish with these thoughts coming into my mind while amidst a world pandemic. People lost their jobs while I received disability and had access to the food bank—another humility I experienced—and the rise of mental illness, addiction, and suicide surpassed the height of any past curve. But, for the first time in my life, I felt worthy of the right to survive and be in the world. After my first hospitalized treatment, I saw humanity in myself. I could feel the tip of self-compassion, and I knew I wanted to heal from hating myself. I kept trying, but I held on to a belief that if I succeeded, it was pretentious of me to show up fully in the world, shining my light. But would it really be arrogant to accept myself—to show up less than perfect, to settle with who I am and what I have to offer right now? And the question remained: *What do I have to offer the world right now?* Arghhhh!

Yes, to this day, I experience anxiety around food, even if my wise mind knows it has never been about the food. The latest has been a way to cope just like any other addiction to soothe, displace, punish, and numb. Those behaviours have been ingrained for so long now; I need to rewire my brain to cope differently. I don't know who I am without my eating disorder's darkness hovering over me, keeping me to myself. It is a vicious cycle that is rarely escaped alone. However, for so long, I thought I could. I wanted to have control over it, control over my body, yet not trusting the latest, and the latter not trusting me. It has been an eternal fight as I was unable to function normally on a regular basis. I could not fulfill my personal self-care needs like eating regular meals, taking a shower, getting dressed, or doing groceries. That is why an in-patient recovery program was a mandatory treatment for me to partake in. I found myself crying more than once at the table, staring at a dish of pasta or dessert, feeling stuck and prisoner to my decision-making. The line I can draw between the feeling of failing and wanting to be successful in my recovery is fine and subtle but also as different as poetry and prose. I definitely know the difference, but it isn't easy to define and articulate.

I began questioning whether I could heal and go into full recovery without the program. Who was I to think I deserved the freedom of being myself and not a chameleon, fitting perfectly within a wall's tapestry? This is the question I constantly ask myself as I debate the pros and cons of recovery. I fully believed the house should have reopened when phase two restrictions were lifted. I wanted support for mental illness to be an essential service. Not only for me in the eating disorders program, but for all the other patients worldwide who were and still are suffering but cannot get help. Overdoses were never as high in British Columbia as in March 2020, with deaths numbering over 100 per month. It is excruciatingly sad to hear of so many people suffering in silence.

As I continued moving through to recovery, I was sad as I body-checked in the mirror to find my body changing into something that did not meet my expectations. I felt I was settling for less and that I was failing at my eating disorders. I am scared because I know the point of treatment is to manage these feelings.

It's unbearable and empowering at the same time. I don't believe I am to blame for the life experiences I lived through. However, I am responsible for healing the wounds that were imposed on me. I often want to scream about the unfairness of my situation, and I am very aware that I am not alone in that process. So many have traumas and issues, including all the distress created by this pandemic. Everyone continues the attempt to repair the damage they struggle with due to Covid-19: financial, emotional, and mental repercussions. It is empowering that for once, I am stepping up to say that I am struggling too.

I continue to struggle with body image distortion and weight gain during this pandemic and the frustration affiliated with this global event as it monopolizes my life. Most of my clothes do not fit me anymore, and I feel uncomfortable in my skin. Wearing a mask might help to be unseen, yet it makes me anxious to wear one. I feel I am being forced to be silent, that my freedom to exist is restricted while living freely is the very thing I have been fighting my entire life for.

As the curve flattened and the second phase was implemented, I was still in my home studio, with seventy percent of the original program completed online. Unfortunately, there was still no date to return to the in-patient facility treatment. I expressed my disbelief and concern to my specialist that people could get their hair done, but our treatment program could not re-open at the house. Although I understood it wasn't as easy as I wished it could be, I again felt that I and my voice didn't matter—nothing had changed. I am not an expert in this area, and I do not know the logistics behind re-opening an in-patient facility, but it felt unfair that mental health treatments were not an essential service.

However, I experienced an awakening. In the past, I would have been passive about the issue and accepted it as it was, but this time, the unbelievable happened as I refused to be a victim and chose to be my own hero. Alongside my peers, I wrote a letter sent to the coordinator of the eating disorder program and the provincial health authority to make my concerns heard—my voice became my sword. My words were my weapon, fighting for my rights and what I believe is my truth. I was able to ask for what I thought was right, not only for me but for the others who were in the same fight as me.

On day 166 of isolation, I was called back to the inpatient treatment centre. Not only that, but I was given an additional five weeks of treatment due to the repercussions of the program being interrupted and because we advocated for ourselves. I experienced great relief and felt victorious.

I had not used symptoms for a long time. And then, one evening, while delaying acting on them, I had a sense of wanting to grasp onto something outside of myself because I was, once again, afraid. I felt like numbing my feelings, and I had not felt that urge in a long time. I could feel every inch of my body expanding, taking up more and more space in the room. I felt my thighs touching each other and my stomach extending in front of me. I felt my body getting larger by the second with the warmth of the pressure of every inch of my legs taking up more space as they kissed my clothes like an invader. My arms felt heavy and jiggly, and my chin was doubling. I was incredibly uncomfortable.

I feel out of control.
I feel alone.
I feel uncomfortable.
I feel out of place.
I feel fat… even though fat is not a feeling.

I was scared. I so wanted to appear like I had my shit together: *I'm fine.* But really, I was not. I never liked my body at any shape or weight, so obviously, it was not better having this added stress. I would have paid anything to go back to where I was before Covid.

I wondered who I was with this new body, trying to navigate life and the world pandemic. Hiding felt like the best solution, but then phase three of restrictions were lifted, and I had to determine how to walk with my head up high. I wondered if people would choose judgment and pity or compassion and empathy: *Don't worry, everybody is gaining weight during the pandemic; it's called COVID Weight!* I felt misunderstood. I am not everybody. I do not want to be everybody.

The extended five weeks of my program went by so quickly. I had to start wearing a mask while cooking to avoid any contagion for either myself or others. Wearing a mask was a constant challenge for me. It made me feel that I could not speak up and express myself as it restricted my breathing. I got dizzy and teary, and the message I perceived was: *Just shut up and endure the situation, whether you like it or not.* It brought me back to past years when I refused to get help, minimizing myself and not wanting to be seen. I felt I was finally making headway, but now I was expected to hide and repress who I am. The irony is that long ago, I set goals of being authentic and assertive, and just when I was finally ready to evolve and show my true self, I was asked to cover my face, nose, and mouth. The beautiful thing is that I now refuse to hide; I have let go of all my masks.

As my jasmine plant bloomed and my recovery program came to an end, I found myself writing my story's final words for a special edition Daring to Share™ Global book—Daring to Share Chaos to Calm: Awakenings Through Covid. I know there is no coincidence. I think of the beautiful timeline speaking to me in a wonderful and subtle way. I do know and feel I have so much more to conquer, to give to the world, to heal, and to learn about how to love. There will be a new storm, a new path, a new vision, and a new battle, but I will also have achieved a new degree of freedom within the ability to choose Chaos or Calm. Eating Disorder or Recovery. Captivity or Freedom. Freedom is the path I want to take.

I have not drowned in the deep waves of the pandemic. Instead, I held on to the raft that life threw at me. I did survive, lived, and really thrived. I found the freedom I craved because I could choose, and I used that choice to discover the art of coming back to life while chaos surged around me. And, just like the world pandemic, this journey of self-discovery has not yet been stamped with an end date on the calendar. However, I learned to use my ability to choose the rhythm of my own galop, my own dance, my own speed, my own path—my own life. This life journey of self-discovery is far from being terminated, yet I feel I have gained a taste of justice, connection, assertiveness, worthiness, peace, grace, purpose, and freedom. I have not totally broken free of all doubts of rejection and fear, and I have not completely solved the complexity of my addiction. However, every morning, I wake up with the ability to choose the direction I want to take.

I always have the freedom to choose, and I want forever to be my own hero and keep feeling the freedom and inner peace

I found in myself. If I no longer live in fear, I am free. And this is something I want to remind myself of every day: I have the choice to experience freedom. With that idea of freedom, I left the house on August 14th, 2020, knowing I would go into the follow-up program. I would start designing the life I want for myself, with its new realities, new challenges, new tools, new wins, new identity acceptance, and peace of mind.

However, there was one more *thing* I needed to explore if I wanted to shed the part of me that resisted stepping into my authentic self and unlocking to another level of the freedom I was seeking…

Hungry to Reveal

I had to come out.

But how does someone officially do their coming out? There is no absolute recipe. I thought about it a hundred times for so many years, and I talked about it in therapy when I was sent home during the confinement for what we all thought would be two weeks. When I was in 4 North West, I brought it up a few times to my care team, my primary nurse, my psychologist, as well as my psychiatrist at Vista—all behind closed doors. I also connected with a lesbian spiritual counsellor before I left. She was doing an internship at 4 North West, and I wanted to ask her for guidelines on how I could start meeting other lesbians while being my authentic self. I wanted to figure out how to do that without hurting anyone's feelings, including mine, and I didn't know how and where to start. I have heard a lot of women wanting to experiment and try to be with another woman. They want to see if it resonates with them or not, but I wanted something to happen organically. I didn't want it to be something that looked or felt like an experiment with someone. And I, especially, didn't want another human being feeling that they were part of an experiment for my benefit; I didn't want anyone to feel used or manipulated in the process.

I definitely wanted to explore my feelings with a professional and have support with my coming out. So, I talked to my psychologist at Vista and shared that I thought I might be gay. It was hard for me because I wondered: *Why do I feel the need to tell anyone that I might be gay?* I thought about it and realized that if I was, I didn't want people around me, or even strangers, to assume I was straight. Again, my real worry was that I was scared my need to be seen as my true self would be perceived as attention-seeking.

After speaking to my psychologist one day, I was filled with emotion and needed to talk to someone who would understand my situation, so I called my friend, John. Even though it was more than two weeks after the original lockdown, I asked him if we could meet outside. He agreed, and we sat two meters apart on chairs in his front yard. His husband, Scott, stood behind him, looking at me with loving eyes—he seemed to know I had something important to share. I was shaking, but I trusted I was in good hands and proceeded to tell him that I was experiencing ambiguity about my sexual identity. I told him that I was questioning what to do and where to start and I felt lost within that process. I will never forget the moment John turned to Scott for approbation, and he responded by coming around to hold and comfort me. And then, John looked me in the eyes: *My dear, I love you, and you are not alone. You are part of the family.*

After I returned home, back in my tiny studio apartment, I felt empowered. Even if I was not ready to start meeting other women and dating—because I wanted to focus on finishing my treatment first—I felt I was planting the seed of becoming much more true to myself. And so, I began peeling off the layers of who I truly am. I was totally ok if I determined I was heterosexual and continued dating men. Still, and more importantly, I needed to go through the process of exploring and expressing what I had been avoiding—discovering my identity.

I was terrified to talk about that subject in my therapy group because I thought my peers might change their perspectives about me. I didn't want to be perceived differently than I had been or rejected right off the bat by people I was starting to have deep connections with. Then one day, I decided to talk about it. I felt silly, creating a huge deal about making an *announcement* that put a lot of focus on me and was really not big news per se. However, to finally make that statement, it was for me. The more I talked about it and mentioned that I wasn't sure, that I didn't really know, etc., etc., I felt more obnoxious putting it out there. But I knew that this *thing* inside of me needed to be extracted so my heart could keep beating, my lungs could remain breathing, and the blood in my veins could continue flowing.

The first time I talked about it with my peers was on a Zoom call during an open talk the week after I confided in my psychologist. We had open talks every Monday morning at ten o'clock. Anyone could bring a topic for discussion—something they went through during the weekend, a question, etc.—and the group would share around that subject. I was afraid my friends wouldn't hug me anymore if they *knew*. I thought they might be afraid I was interested in them and thus reluctant to hang out with me when we returned to the house after this Covid thing ended. However, the outcome was positive, and I felt so humbled, grateful, and loved after I spoke my truth with it being well-received—I am aware it is not easy for some to talk about their sexuality.

I had so many questions myself: How does someone transition from being heterosexual to homosexual? Is there even such a thing? Was I bi or just curious? My confusion reiterated that there is no *how-to* manual navigating and determining one's gender. For me, it wasn't about *that*, but more about people not assuming I was one or another. Maybe I was bisexual…I didn't like the terminology or labels; I don't like to put myself in categories or boxes, especially when I'm not absolutely sure of *what* I am. I was sure that I needed to explore that beyond a therapeutic room with my psychologist because that was only the first step. It was important for me to confirm who I am by experiencing what love looked and felt like with my heart. Of course, all this stirred up some issues I was previously unable to admit to regarding my identity and sexuality, but it also helped me consider that it might be time to bring them to the table—or at least start contemplating them. I also told myself that I would find my *Ellen*—Portia de Rossi's wife—whether it was a man or a woman. But, for some reason, I was leaning towards her being a woman!

During the six months I was home doing my online long-distance treatment, I moved to the small town of Comox, British Columbia in Canada. After my last bit of treatment in Vancouver, I was ready to return home to my new apartment in the Comox Valley. I chose this shared apartment because it was close to the pier and the water, which was what I was looking for. In addition, everything was within walking distance: the grocery store, a used bookstore and coffee shop—anything I needed was right there.

**A deep sense of assuredness and conviction
within my soul motivated me to move there.
My higher self was constantly, but softly and lovingly,**

whispering a secret in my ear,
reminding me what my next step was.
I tuned in and welcomed the information I was given
and accepted the guidance life gave.

Journal Entry
April 16, 2020

Where should I move? Comox, Tofino, or Port Alberni? I am constantly hearing in my head that I should move to Comox. So, I think I will listen to that because the feeling I get is too strong to avoid.

Journal Entry
April 22, 2020

My tears are fluid and as passionate as the watershed finding its way into the stream. My tears are cold like the spring rain, confused about the direction they should take and the temperature they should be. My tears run fast on my skin like the speed the stream allows the fresh water to travel from rock to rock, finding its way in between obstacles and against any hardships. Despite the seasons and the weather and rocks, the fresh water from the mountains always finds its way to meet the river, just like my salted tears will find their way from my eyes to my cheeks, to my chest, to the truth.

Once I moved into my new house before going back to treatment in Vancouver, I went on a couple of dates with women I met online. Nothing *clicked* in that we were not looking for similar things in a relationship, and I felt in my heart that none of them provided what I was genuinely looking for. I know for sure that I wanted the comfort of knowing I was on the right track—that I could be or appear like a lesbian. But in the end, these connections didn't feel authentic. I believed I was still seeking validation similar to my past relationships, so I recognized that I wasn't ready to move ahead in that direction yet. I decided to postpone my search for my sexual identity until after my treatment, so it would be more heartfelt and not based on my ego; it was too important to me that searching for a partner was in line with my values. I didn't want to repeat the same mistakes I made in the past. So, with that mindset, I went back to treatment in July 2020 for five more weeks.

I was indeed looking forward to graduating from my treatment at the Vista House. I would have stayed longer, but new residents were starting to move in, and I was used to my intimate group of people—we knew each other so well. I was ready to go home, and despite not knowing how things would go or how navigating new paths and waters would be, I looked forward to the beginning of building a life using the abilities I acquired. I didn't want to be cocky, but I was sure I would do well, if not great. However, I had such a hard time admitting that to myself. My inner critic always came back at me, asking: *Who do you think you are?*

Journal Entry
August 14, 2020

We were asked to write a recovery letter to our eating disorder from our follow-up psychologist:

This is not the first time I am writing you a letter to talk about our relationship, and hopefully, this time around will be the last.

Although I have a firm and strong desire to live my life without you, I have never fully believed in recovery. Yes, I had a glimpse it could be real. I had a glimpse of light shining towards the direction of healing, but my tank is now full: I feel I have reached the amount of learning for this time around. I am confused, but I am also trying to be resilient. All this time, I thought treatment would heal me completely, especially going over the initially planned 15 weeks. Although Covid-19 sucks, I feel lucky that it allowed me to receive full support for an extended period of time. I thought my treatment would heal me completely—it's part of my perfectionistic personality to want to succeed, check boxes, and conquer adversity, and I feel a bit defeated—by you. You are very tenacious; I have to give you that. You are strong. You are determined. But so am I. Yes, my tank is full right now, and I feel I have learned the capacity of what I can. I don't think I can learn anymore, and it's time to go into the real world to use my treatment tools. I have learned what I had to for this moment in time. I thought I would be instantly happy when I graduated, but now that the journey is over at Vista, I am scared.

The first few weeks of follow-up were hard. I felt a bit left alone, navigating life without the program. My body had changed, and I wasn't comfortable with it. Because we were in confinement due to the pandemic, I couldn't have people come to see me. So, I decided to visit my family in Montreal, and I was scared to do so because I was fearful someone would comment on my weight gain. I also almost cancelled a camping trip with a friend because I didn't want to show up in a bathing suit in front of her—I knew my mind would start comparing our physiques, and I didn't want to be in that mind space with her.

Upon my return from Montreal, I was immensely relieved to be back in my follow-up group, receiving support because I had returned to overeating and felt that no matter what I ate, my body was expanding; I wanted to go back to hiding and isolating. During the last few weeks of my follow-up treatment, one of the girls in my group passed away. It felt extremely unreal. One week, she was struggling, and a week later, she wasn't with us anymore. I never knew what happened, and it is not important, but her death did hit me—it could have been any of the girls in treatment that week. It also could have been me. Eating disorders are deadly, whether someone dies due to organ failure or the mental illness that drives them to commit suicide. It is raw, it is awful, but it is the truth. And honestly, I never thought about it when I was restricting, either overeating or over-exercising.

Every time I came back from treatment, I thought I was healed, yet nothing seemed to have changed from the last time. When I arrived home in March 2020, I had the same hope. I assumed that after seven months, my struggle with my eating disorder would be over because that is what I do—I get shit done, and I achieve. However, what I didn't understand was that acquiring that magnitude of wisdom requires rest and quiet. I needed to allow myself to communicate with my inner child and my future self, as well as the Julie who existed in between, so I could align with my heart—with who I was in the present. I was floating in the distraction of self-improvement, wanting to be a better person but not stopping the pattern that got in the way of my evolution; I was healing but also wanted to lose weight and I wasn't satisfied with my body image. However, the treatment was proving to be successful, as well as terrifying because it was so new to me.

When I got home on August 14th, 2020, I wanted to

delete the dating app I was using at the time. I didn't want to focus on relationships anymore, whether heterosexual or homosexual, other than the one I had with myself. I had a deep desire to strengthen the connection I had with myself and focus positively on recovery. However, as a curious person, I decided to have one last look before removing the app for good. I knew it was contrary to my intention, but I couldn't help myself, taking one more chance to find a new person in my area who might actually be a good fit. So, although I wanted to get rid of my account, I did one *last swipe* before doing so. When I did, a super fun woman I met in Club Med Colorado in 2006 popped up. She had apparently moved to Comox as well! We were coworkers back then, and we both believed we were *straight*. Even though we didn't spend much time together, we got along well, and she was enjoyable to be with. So, after the infamous *swipe*, we decided to video-chat for a few minutes and meet to catch-up upon my return from a trip to Montreal.

I was leaving a few days later to visit family there for 3 weeks. I was excited to reconnect with Kay, but never I never thought it would be the beginning of a fantastic adventure with the woman of my dreams—my *Ellen*! It started with a friendship and then quickly developed into a beautiful sentimental and romantic relationship. The more we spent time together, I discovered how beautiful this woman was from the inside out. Yes, I was scared because my body was different than when she knew me before. I had adopted a healthy weight considering what I was going through at that time, and although I deeply wanted to be loved for who I truly was and not only for my external appearance, I wanted her to find me attractive. I wanted her to find me attractive despite my weight gain—the weight my body seemed to always remember, similar to Portia de Rossi when she mentions in her book that she was her heaviest when she met Ellen. That part of her story helped me navigate the uneasiness I carried with my new body just as Portia de Rossi did. I always hold onto the hope of this part of her story: that from her lowest point, after she started to ascend the agonizing climb to a healthy and honest life, she fell in love and married Ellen DeGeneres. Because of the hope her words instilled in me, I didn't have the slightest doubt that one day, I would also find my *Ellen*. And...I did.

However, I still struggled with the lingering ambiguity of accepting both the feminine and masculine sides of my being—the Ying and the Yang. I always felt pressured by society, dictating that I should present externally as feminine. But when I abided by those ultra-feminine standards by putting a dress or a lot of makeup on, I was like a bull in a china shop. I always preferred to wear just a slight touch of makeup with a counterbalance of a more neutral masculine look. I remember seeing a picture of myself wearing a white dress standing in the kitchen of the house I grew up in. It had white walls and navy-blue kitchen drawers—the dramatic contrast of the deep blue tone evoked sensations of conformity of power, importance, and authority.

Along with the navy doors and drawers, two walls had matching wallpaper with a tapestry of white and blue checkers. Wicker baskets stood out prominently on one wall. I remember this kitchen as if I was standing in it yesterday. I also have a photo of myself mimicking the ballerina on one of my birthday cakes. I'm wearing a white crochet dress that my mother made—she loved making her daughters' clothes. Every time I look at this picture, I empathize with this little girl, trying to pose for the camera, imitating a dancer, trying to be perfectly cute, but simultaneously feeling awkward in that dress. I always had a hard time embracing the feminine side of me. Wearing dresses and being all done up never really resonated with me, but I had this ingrained perception I needed to provide this façade in order to get compliments and feel safe—to be accepted.

Kay seduced me with her confidence about who she is. She embraces her masculinity, her strength, and her uniqueness. I will never forget the day I knew I was falling in love with her: she was wearing a red and white plaid shirt, her Blundstone boots, black, work cargo pants, and she stood before me with her hands in her pockets. We were about to go for a stroll in the woods, and she wanted to change my mind because I wasn't feeling well that day because I was feeling self-conscious about the way I looked. But Kay held space for me and gently listened to how I felt, receiving what I had to say without minimizing my thoughts or emotions. She gave me a hug, and as she held me in her arms, she comforted my hurting soul. At that moment, something changed. The chaos of wondering if my body was appealing or not was gone, and our souls connected. From that moment, I felt from deep within that she saw me for who I am, and I wanted to kiss her.

The horse stopped abruptly, landing on his back legs
while lifting its forward legs in the air,
and I extend my swords toward the sky.
It is foggy, and I can barely see through the clouds.
I hear them walking towards me.
The horse jolts back on all four feet.
The wolves approach so close that I hear their warm breath
as precise and distinct as if they are whispering in my ear;
the humidity of their breath and smoke
from their mouth is palpable.
I come down off my horse,
offering my hand towards the pack leader's nose,

so, it can smell me—so it can tame me, and I can tame it.
As I caress the soft fur of what I thought was my enemy,
my heartbeat slows down.
Its eyes become softer as it smells my hand and looks at me
with tenderness. With forgiveness.
With Love. Understanding. Compassion. Empathy.
We came a long way,
and we have further to go before we truly know each other.
But, for now, we choose to set each other free.

I have learned that I have moved through a lifetime of transformation. It's a mutation that continues to provide many blessings. I discovered that I can't be concerned with endings, and my prayers will always be answered—all changes are for the best. I am excited for the gifts yet to be offered as I release the old and make space for the new. I am embracing hunger, displacing my old identity and value of sex, weight, and shape. There was a time when death was the contemplation of my desire. My goal was to end the battle of being trapped within my identity of self-hatred because I didn't know I had the choice to be my own hero...until I did and took ownership of the choices before me. It was time to reconsider society's values and how I wanted to edit my life, presenting myself authentically while positively influencing others as a role model, fighting pseudo standards of beauty.

From the moment I began dating Kay, I was finally free to scream that I loved a woman to the world. I was openly with a woman, and although our relationship was new, I knew she was the one from the moment we kissed that very first day. That definitely freaked her out, but I had no doubt and still don't to this day. Finally, I was ready to welcome unconditional love into my life—the unquestionable. One week after we started dating, I started calling my family to begin *coming out* and telling them I had a partner. I couldn't wait. Yes, she was the first woman I ever committed to, and maybe we would only last a few weeks, but I was so relieved I was finally letting go of my secret. I was coming out, and I didn't care how new our relationship was! I started by sharing with a few close friends and then with my therapy group. Then I told my sister. And then my father, my brother, and lastly, my mother. I made most of my announcements by video calls because I wanted to make it as personal as possible, given the distance between us.

Each time I shared who I really am and my newfound love, I cried overwhelming tears of joy in response to the positivity and love I received in return. I discovered that whoever I am and whoever I love, the people in my life were happy for me and cheered me on. One day while sitting in Kay's truck, I found myself crying and feeling strange due to all the love I received and surrounded me. All those years, I didn't realize all the people who supported me. Because of all the chatter in my brain, I focused on busily trying to disassociate from my inner pain by constantly hurting my body through the use of my eating disorder. I never saw the amount of love that surrounded me because I was completely distracted from the truth.

When I looked back on my journal entry of April 28, 2020, I recognized how the little girl in me wanted to protect herself from the story she had created in her head so long ago...

I am looking at my newborn picture. The first picture that was taken of me.

Dear world...
Dear world....
Did I see it coming?
What happened?

Her fingers are so tiny—I can almost see them moving, expressing her excitement to be born. Her mouth looks like a heart, and her eyes are still, oh so, very dark—a beautiful dark blue like that of the depths of the sea. I see her fragility, this delicate little human being whose destiny is to be happy, to spread joy, love, and healing energy around her.

What does she think of her new world, discovering the light outside of her mother's womb?

I am looking at that beautiful baby girl—she is me. Little did I know what the world and life had in store for me, how the experiences of my life from the very first day I saw the world would shape me.

Little did I know that one day, amid of a world pandemic and panic, I would look at this beautiful picture of the first hour of my life and try to connect the dots to draw the portrait of who I am today—that I would try to connect that baby to the woman I am in this present moment.

I wish I could hold that baby in my arms and tell her that I love her as she holds my index finger with her tiny hand. I wish I could rock her as she looks into the depth of my eyes that attempt to understand why I am so moved by her beauty and innocence. I wish she knew that I genuinely wanted her to be happy, to be held and loved; so, so much.

If only I could warm her with my love, so she would never be cold. I would support her with the love in my eyes, looking deep into hers. My love for her would make her feel strong enough to conquer the world with the confidence of knowing and never doubting for a second that she was born for greatness, being exactly who she is.

Hungry to Love

Tears of perplexity fall down my face each time I read that latest passage in my journal, as well as when I look at a picture of me as a baby or young child. I can't look at them for too long because it honestly hurts my heart. I see the love this child is. I see the beauty this child is. I see the humanity this child is.

Nonetheless, I cannot explain what happened that motivated me to hate the adult I became. I would never want to hurt that child by making her feel unworthy, unloved, hated, or go through what I have lived. And yet, I made it happen. I am still befuddled by how much I dissociated to the point whereby I ended up hating her—I accepted and believed she could never be good enough. I sincerely want to apologize to her for what she endured so she can finally go out into the world, living and feeling the joy she deserves to experience.

It is equally time for me to let go of the guilt and shame of having been unfair to her because I now know the expanded love and warmth I have and want for that child. I still want joy and greatness for her, and although I have discovered a little bit more about who I am, I know I still have a lot of work to do to maintain that level of love and remember that I do have that amount of love for that child.

I always truly and fully wanted to be at peace with myself—I just never knew how. Even after almost two years of treatment and therapy, I still have so much to unpack and go through to discover the full portrait of who I know I am from deep within. I never really knew what I was on this Earth for because I couldn't allow myself to live joyfully or be totally satisfied with anything I achieved.

However, for once in my life, I have certainty that I am on the right path, that I am now *living the purpose* the angel talked about while I laid unconscious in the snow decades ago. For once in my life, I am serene and content with the direction life is taking me. I am not looking for *more*. Instead, I am at peace with my decisions; choosing to pursue and embrace my relationship with Karine—Kay—is definitely one of the best decisions I ever made, along with moving back to Quebec where I was born. We moved to a beautiful small town on the east coast that borders mountains and the Atlantic sea, exactly where I spent my summers when I was a young child. It reminds me of Comox, where I met Karine and that I loved so much with the same smell of algae and water I experienced on Vancouver Island, reminding me of the salt waters of my childhood. Moving from one coast to another for the second time has provided a space where I feel at home—finally! Karine and I bought a beautiful piece of land that belonged to my mother's sister, an aunt I used to spend time with at my grandparents' place during summers in beautiful Gaspésie. She is the one who used to comfort me any time I missed my parents, and she helped me dial the number on the rotary phone hanging on the wall. I wanted to hear their voices and needed reassurance that they were coming back to pick me up from my grandparents at the end of summer vacation.

I have so many good memories of the time I spent with my aunts during their young university years. We used to go to the beach, throw rocks in the calm sea, and watch the ripples they created on the water. We jumped over orange jellyfish on the shore and named them *sun of the sea*. I remember loving being close to the water, breathing in the fresh salt air and odour that wafted off the barrachois—a sandbar that creates a lagoon separated from the ocean when the tide is low. We had campfires in the brick pit between the trees and spent time with my cousins at their father's farm, making and staking hay ballots into the barn and feeding and milking the cows while listening to the song *Kokomo* by the Beach Boys at five in the morning. While I hung one of my aunt's clothes on the line, I imagined having a big family of five kids one day. It was at the same time I decided I didn't need a husband and would rather be inseminated like my uncle's cows! As much as I missed my parents when I was there, I remember being filled with the love my grandparents and aunts washed over me.

Returning to this place I now call home as I slowly come back to myself, I am finally curious and learning what it really means to say: *I am coming home.*

Coming home to my body, to the person I am,
Coming back to oneself,
For myself, for my health,
For nobody else.

I travelled to many countries as a flight attendant for 13 years. I backpacked on my own through Indonesia and Nicaragua. And after having moved more than 20 times in less than 15 years, I have learned that *home* is really within oneself. *Home* was the only variable as I travelled from chaos to calm, from suffering to liberation, from self-hate to self-love, from captivity to freedom, from doubt to hope, from darkness to light, and eventually from fatality to being my own hero—life has brought me full circle, back to my beautiful home. I unconsciously came back to where I was most happy during my youth, alongside a partner I share unconditional love with.

Yes, I recently moved back to Quebec, where it all began. I went back to a place where the same joy and love I craved my whole life has rested in my heart since I was a young child. It is where the St. Lawrence River meets the Atlantic Ocean and where I wore my favourite red swimsuit with the ruffles at the collar as I danced many times in the rain on the front lawn of my grandparents' house when a storm hit. I loved being under the water, feeling and tasting the drops that landed on my tongue. I had such a thirst for life, feeling so alive as I danced with the music I invented in my head, experiencing second after second of pure joy. I was just seven years old, and the grass tickled my bare feet as I spun around and around until I got dizzy and needed to stop. I often climbed the cherry tree with my grandfather's wooden ladder, filling huge buckets so my grandmother could make cherry jam and cookies—ah, the smell of her baking. My grandmother tucked me into bed every night after we climbed the staircase to my summer room. I prayed at night, hoping that the Earth would not break in two—a prayer that my grand-mother loved me reciting—so my parents could get to me and pick me up at the end of the summer with my siblings.

I have moved to my mother's birthplace, travelling the path of her youth, scrolling on the same beaches, walking the same streets of her teenage and young adult life. I am witnessing the same sea and looking up to the same clouds and moon on a clear evening as it reflects off the water like a mirror of her life. It always comes back to the mother—my mother's blood. Red. The colour of suffering when one hurts and bleeds, but also the colour of passion and love. The vision of the relationship I now have with my mother is so different than it used to be. I cannot live within regrets, but if I knew back then, I would have asked questions long before I had all too recently. I would have asked my mother about her story before I interpreted the only version I knew—that of my own story. I would have cleared the story in my head that I had of her for so long. I would have told her how I felt instead of building a fence between us. I often asked myself: *Was that perception real*, or *was it an illusion?*

In August 2020, I sensed our relationship significantly shifting when I went back to Montreal after my last treatment. She asked me questions and mentioned how she felt—I could see she cared. The moment this realization hit me was when she insisted on driving me to the airport, and she didn't want to cry. At that time, I told her it was okay to be vulnerable and to express her emotions. When she finally allowed her tears to roll from her beautiful deep sea-blue eyes onto her cheeks, I was pacified with a huge weight lifted off my shoulders and chest. I believe she has been suffering all this time—maybe all her life too—about something I have never known. Maybe she tried to reach out to me, but I was too young to understand. I did not consciously know what she wanted to tell me during that visit as she stood before me, releasing her despair through her tears, but my soul understood this time, and I immediately made peace with what I had perceived as a war between us for so long. Since then, we have been communicating more authentically, and she seems really happy that I have moved back to Quebec and where she grew up.

My mother sent me an email the other day, telling me that she envisioned me walking the path of her young adult life, walking on the same beaches and frequenting the same places she did when she lived in the area as a young child and woman. Funnily enough, she will be moving back here as well next year. We lived separately in different countries for so many years, but now, we will be closer—physically, and I believe emotionally—than we have been in a long time.

The relationship between my father and I has never been so great. After all these years, I know that he is very proud of who I have become, and he loves the idea of me being loved and cared for within a relationship. Being as sensitive as he is, he greeted Kay with so much warmth and love. I feel blessed that he was so receptive, accepting her with open arms—Kay, the person I love the most in the entire world.

Kay! My *Ellen*! Our relationship took big steps forward really fast. I do not like labels or stereotypes, but I can humbly and humorously say that we U-Hauled pretty fast on that one… However, the love we have for each other is so strong and real that I truly believe it is the definition of unconditional love. We accept and respect each other for who we genuinely are, along with both our flaws and qualities. We complete each other so well; she is my Yang, and I am her Yin. And I have never felt so complete with anyone else.

I often get asked about my sexual orientation because I have dated men in the past and I am not in denial or shy to talk about it. For example, I often get asked if I always knew I was a lesbian and attracted to women. Do I identify as a lesbian? A bisexual? A queer? I am entirely honest when I say that I do not have definite answers to these questions. I have intentionally tried not to label myself my entire life, and I continue to carry the same mindset now. What I do know is that the love I share with Kay is unconditional, and there is one thing I am certain about, which is that I am immensely grateful to be living in a time where being in a relationship with someone of the same sex is possible. I am beyond thankful for those before me who lead the way for all of us to live free and openly, no matter our gender. To be clear, even though things are better on the inclusion front, society generally has a long way to go. It is still not always easy, but every time I am out with my girlfriend, I am fortunate to experience the same joy I felt when I came out the very first time. My family provides so much love and acceptance to both Kay and me, and I know that I am privileged and extremely lucky because I am conscious that not all coming out stories have a positive outcome—I have heard heartbreaking confessions about others who deserve the same peace that I have been given. To them, I send so much love.

I see my quest to be my own hero as a rite of passage from who I pretended to be to remembering who I am authentically. It encompassed exiting the dark night of my soul to provide the space to be reborn closer to the person I want to be—from suffering to hate to fear to faith to acceptance to love.

> *You may be blind to the very thing that will*
> *make your life feel worth living.*
> *You may be repressing the very source*
> *of your deepest satisfaction.*
> *You may be gullible, taking in the world's*
> *Insidious lessons in superficial satisfaction.*
> *Therefore, you have to dig deeper.*
> *Discover who you are and who you want to be.*
> *Don't be dissuaded from that objective by the*
> *illusory promise of commercial life.*
> *Instead, be yourself.*[13]

---

[13] Thomas Moore, Dark night of the Soul, p.19, Gotham Books, 2004/

The horse and the wolves have learned to cohabitate in the same body without dissociating. I need to be mindful of how I talk to myself, how I see myself, and how I treat myself. This allows me to recognize the triggers and use the tools I have learned in the past two years. Since I am mentally unable to unlearn what I know now, I still don't own a scale and even though it is tempting as hell, I know it won't benefit me to have one. I do not have a big mirror, so I cannot see my entire self. When times get hard, I always come back to the reasons why I asked for help in the first place, and I remember that I do not want to go back to where I was before I was hospitalized.

Recovery is certainly not a perfectly traced lane, and I know that keeping my eating disorders close is a way to self-destruct as an excuse to not to reach my full potential. Deep inside my heart, I want to succeed in getting myself to a better place and fully accepting who I am. I want to inspire others to be themselves and believe that their existence matters—we all matter. Again, I had this choice to make: *Did I want to stay in my own victim pity party, or did I want to be my own hero and live the life I always wanted to live?* There was only one option: to be my own hero.

No holds barred; recovery is not linear. It is not black and white. I have been warned since day one, but I didn't want to believe it. I thought it would be either one or the other, either stuck in the prison of my eating disorders or healed by the freedom from them. Honestly, I am in a grey zone—and grey is okay! I know I have worked hard, and I know I still have work to do, but what is important is that I am doing the work—progression over perfection. Again, recovery is not linear, it is fluctuating, and this is the reality of my situation. I cannot tell you that I am entirely healed or that I have conquered my eating disorder completely. However, I am confident that I am now able to manage my thoughts, emotions, and urges in a healthier way. Acting on my eating disorder symptoms is not a synonym of victory for me anymore. I do not feel superior or *high* if I want to act on symptoms; it is actually the opposite.

I still have self-sabotaging thoughts about my body image, but I can manage them using the tools and practices I have been given to serve me. When I feel those thoughts approaching, I see them, acknowledge them, and question them: *Where are they coming from? How do I feel at this present moment? What just happened that is making me feel like I am not worthy? Do I have too much on my plate? Why do I feel like I want to dissociate? Am I overwhelmed? Did I eat enough today?* I acknowledge the urge and the desire to act on them, but I now know myself better, so I can show up with the knowledge I learned during my stays at St-Paul's and Discovery Vista—I can't unlearn what I have learned there.

I now live within balance with the strength of both the horse and the wolves. Living with both dualities as companions—the horse and the wolf pack now coexist. The balance of dualism within these two personalities coexisting inside of myself provides me with enormous strength. I recognize I have to be mindful of my triggers because at any time, the primal drive in the wolves can resurface without any warning. It is the horse's responsibility to be alert and keep its hooves planted firmly on the ground, avoiding being stepped on by the power of the wolves. Just like the horse needs to stand its ground not to be taken over by the wolves, so do the wolves need to step back to honour the horse's presence. Each is strong in their own right, but they are more empowered when working together.

For me, the following combination creates balance:

Inner peace;
Inner Guidance;
Self-trust;
Freedom;
Equanimity.

I can see and envision where I am right now,
in a beautiful leafy garden,
where I, the horse, and the wolves cohabitate.
I see myself lying in the beautiful meadow
between the horse and the wolves.
I am content.
I wear my sword, reminding me that I am a fighter,
as well as a peacemaker,
but from now on, I will fight for myself and be forever
an advocate for recovery.
The sun lightens the garden with its beautiful golden rays.
It is warm and peaceful.
I savour life with my eyes closed,
trusting and empowered.
But every so often, I take a look at the horizon,
being vigilant, knowing that
a storm can approach at any time.
I keep an eye of diligence on the wolves,
reminding myself that their divine nature is wild,
and I can never change that.
I have the horse by my side, who can now stand its ground
and carry me wherever I need to go.
And I have me.
I will always make sure that I stay true to myself,
so that never again will I be
Hungry to be Me.

Bibliography

American Family Physician, https://nedic.ca/
eating-disorders-treatment/anorexia-nervosa/

Canada Suicide Prevention Service, 1-833-456-4566, https://
www.crisisservicescanada.ca/en/

Crisis Services Canada, https://www.crisisservicescanada.ca/
en/looking-for-local-resources-support

de Rossi, Portia. Unbearable lightness: A Story of Loss and
Gain. New York: Atria Books, 2011.

Goodreads, www.goodreads.com/book/
show/9219901-unbearable-lightness

Kelty Mental Health Resource
Center, www.keltyeatingdisorders.ca/
vista-eating-disorders-treatment-program

Moore, Thomas. Dark night of the Soul: Gotham Books,
2004, p. 19.

National Eating Disorder Information Centre (NEDIC),
https://nedic.ca/eating-disorders-treatment/anorexia-nervosa

Provincial Adult Tertiary Eating Disorders Program,
www.mh.providencehealthcare.org/programs/
provincial-adult-tertiary-eating-disorders-program

Psychiatric Times, www.psychiatrictimes.com/view/
patient-resistance-eating-disorders

Pub Med, www.pubmed.ncbi.nlm.nih.gov/18253742

Reyers, Diana. Daring to Share Chaos to Calm: Awakenings
Through Covid. British Columbia: Daring to Share™
Global, 2020. https://www.daringtoshare.com/chaos-to-calm

Science Direct, https://www.sciencedirect.com/science/
article/pii/B9780128039687000046

Smith, Fran. "The addicted Brain," National Geographics,
September 2017, p. 42,
www.nationalgeographic.com/magazine/issue/
september-2017

CPSIA information can be obtained
at www.ICGtesting.com
Printed in the USA
LVHW031801241121
704372LV00014B/1169